Places in the World a Person Could Walk

Places

in the World a Person Could Walk

Family, Stories, Home,
and Place in the
Texas Hill Country

BY DAVID SYRING

UNIVERSITY OF TEXAS PRESS, AUSTIN

Copyright © 2000 by the University of Texas Press
All rights reserved
Printed in the United States of America
First edition, 2000

Requests for permission to reproduce material from this work should be sent to Permissions, University of Texas Press, P.O. Box 7819, Austin, TX 78713–7819.

∞ The paper used in this book meets the minimum requirements of ANSI/NISO Z39.48–1992 (R1997) (Permanence of Paper).

Library of Congress Cataloging-in-Publication Data

Syring, David, 1967–
    Places in the world a person could walk : family, stories, home, and place in the Texas Hill Country / by David Syring — 1st ed.
        p.   cm.
    Includes bibliographical references (p.   ).
    ISBN 0-292-77746-9 (alk. paper)—ISBN 0-292-77754-x (pbk. : alk. paper)
        1. Texas Hill Country (Tex.)—Social life and customs.   2. Texas Hill Country (Tex.)—Biography.   3. Texas Hill Country (Tex.)—History, Local.   4. Country life—Texas—Texas Hill Country.   5. Family—Texas—Texas Hill Country.   6. Home—Texas—Texas Hill Country.   7. Place (Philosophy)   8. Syring Family.   9. German Americans—Texas—Texas Hill Country.   I. Title.
    F392.T47 S9   2000
    976.4—dc21

                                                                            00-023487

Jacket and cover photographs of McClusky paintings by Frank Minogue.

In gratitude to my family and teachers, and in loving memory of John D. McClusky and Marion Williamson.

Contents

ACKNOWLEDGMENTS   ix

INTRODUCTION:
Dreams and Stories, Fragments and Memories   1

PART 1:
Speaking in Tongues, Telling Tales: Family Stories   15

PART 2:
Honey Creek Church: Chapter and Verse   79

PART 3:
Migrations toward Home: Fredericksburg, Texas   99

PART 4:
Closings: Beginning Again   181

BIBLIOGRAPHY   187

Acknowledgments

Many people have shared insights that helped me write this book. The Syring family in general, and Herbert and Barbara Syring in particular, invited me into the clan and helped me find direction in my questioning. Without their storytelling, this work would not exist. Neither would it exist without the many people who spent time and shared stories with me throughout the Hill Country. Especially important to my understanding of the complexities of the place have been Lois and John McClusky, Terry Theis, Judy Starks, Julia Jarrell, and Carroll Smith.

The group of anthropology graduate students at Rice University that I lived in the midst of when this work first began taking shape also challenged me to pursue the line of thinking that led to this book. I am grateful to them as well, including especially Mitra Emad, Laura Helper, Mazyar Lotfalian, and Christopher Pound, all of whom gave me encouragement (and occasionally places to sleep) at key moments. For creating a unique, stimulating, and supportive intellectual environment I will be forever grateful to the Rice University anthropology department, and especially George Marcus.

I would be remiss if I did not here acknowledge that the title of this book derives from Janet Kauffman's fine first collection of fiction, *Places in the World a Woman Could Walk*. Her unique voice helped me find my own.

Many, many people have written about the Hill Country at length, and works by John Graves, Terry and Gilbert Jordan, Elroy Bode, The Gillespie County Historical Society, and others have been useful as guideposts and sources of voices other than my own. As is evident from my frequent use of quotations from these and other writers, I relish the storied nature of the place.

Edge Falls on Curry Creek.

Introduction

DREAMS AND STORIES, FRAGMENTS AND MEMORIES

Where do we belong when the map of our world has been redrawn; who are our communities; what is the place of family?

Angelika Bammer, "Mother Tongues and Other Strangers,"
Displacements: Cultural Identities in Question

Looking for Home

One day I awoke with an image I had just dreamed. I saw my great uncle, an old Texas-German farmer named Alfred, cutting his neighbor's hair. He tilted this man's head gently to one side and carefully snipped off stray locks, like he was trimming flower stems. The neighbor's young son watched and waited his turn on the steps nearby. I'd heard that Alfred used to do that—cut his neighbor's hair—but the dream image was so clear it was as if I were sitting on the porch with them. I swear, there was a tenderness in the way Alfred's gnarly fingers worked the comb through that man's hair. It was a little like a caress. I could make a whole story out of that gesture. There was something like digging in the soil to make things grow—Alfred's hands moving there. It said something about living in one place so long that even your neighbor's head becomes part of the landscape, known and shaped by your own hands.

In my dream, a young boy watches, almost bored, but waiting. That boy, whose name is Clinton, is now over sixty-five years old, and his face is creased and sun-scorched. The man with the scissors, Uncle Alfred, never married. Until his death a few years ago, he lived on the family homestead with his unmarried sister, Frieda.

I met Clinton one day when I drove to the small piece of property that I call "the shack," and my aunts and uncles call "the country place." It is the difference between those who lived here once, and one who only visits.

It's not much of a thing, this country place. The shack—the building my father lived in with some of his dozen brothers and sisters and their father—was never much, and has become both less and more through years of neglect. It has decayed into nothing but a place for the storage of things no longer useful in the endless flow of everyday life—an old cabinet, rusted bed springs, broken shovels, half-rotted paintings, memories.

These last things, the memories the shack contains, make it more than it once was. Some buildings contain memory as well as boards and nails. My grandfather built this place from cedar posts and wood torn off bomb crates from the air force base in San Antonio. Two of my uncles own it now; they bought it from my grandfather when he was dying of cancer. The family had moved away from the country place many years earlier, because feeding thirteen children on the wages of a fence builder had been simply impossible.

I'm using these names and telling these stories as if I've always known them, as if they are part and parcel of my past, but let me tell you, they're not. They're fragments of a possible past. I might have grown up with Clinton's kids as cousins, if the world were other than it is. But since it is the way it is, I have only story fragments to work with when I try to understand how life in relationship to a place unfolds.

We sat, Clinton and I, on the tailgate of my truck and looked out beyond the shack toward the dry grass of the Burn while we talked.

"I sure did have a sweet spot for your aunt," he said.

"Which one?"

"Virginia. I was sweet on Virginia. We went out once, and I always looked for excuses to come over here to see her." He looked off with tears in his eyes. "I guess we might have been married," he said. "At least I'd have liked to marry her. But then they all moved away. To town. Too far."

My grandfather and his children moved forty miles away, to New Braunfels. I think about the fact that the woman I married was born in Austria, traveled back and forth with her parents to Iran, where her father was born, and grew up mostly in a small town outside Chicago. Clinton and I do not live in the same world—our terms of time and place are utterly different. Yet, I still feel a pull, the yearning to live in one place thoroughly. Clinton has lived that way all his life. I have not lived in one place for more than a decade at a time, and it is possible that I never will. So what can a sense of place possibly mean for my life? What can it mean for so many of us cut loose from easy access to markers such as long-term residence and landownership that are conventionally thought of as the wellsprings of emplacedness?

When I returned to the Hill Country, I hunted, I thought, for some kind of connection to my history—shadowy patterns of the past of my family and its relation to this place. A great-great-uncle once served fifteen years as pastor for the old Catholic church in Fredericksburg. He died, still pastoring, the year I was born. My father almost married a woman from Fredericksburg. Many of my aunts, uncles, and cousins still live in the cities at the edge of the region. In many ways, I felt as if this area belonged, in some small way, to me—or more accurately, I belonged to it.

I *have* found some of that connection to past and place, but it has not been the simple sort of homecoming or return story often told by tellers with a simple "nostalgic" voice. In a 1966 television program designed to introduce then-president Lyndon Johnson's home region—the same area I am writing about—to the rest of the nation, a reporter asked: "What does all this land you see here, Mr. President—what does all this mean to you?" Johnson answered: "Well, the sun seems to be a little brighter, the climate a little warmer, the air a little fresher, the people a little kinder, and more understanding. I guess it is a good deal in what you are accustomed to. . . . I guess we all like home. Maybe I like it a little more than the average fellow."

My experience in the Hill Country coincides, at least superficially, with Johnson's description. When I first looked for a place to live in Fredericksburg, the small town at the region's center, the owners of a local realty gave me a bag of delicious pears from their orchard as a welcoming gift, despite the fact that I had already told them I'd found a place with another real estate agent. They weren't trying to buy a customer; they were welcoming a new neighbor.

But the easy relationship to place and people suggested by Johnson's words and that bag of pears does not provide an adequate basis for me to understand my own relationship to place. Too many of the markers that usually define place are fragmented in my life. I can hear a story about the way that two old farmers used to cut one another's hair, but I'll never sit on that porch myself. In an age of mobility, when the members of many families don't even live in the same state, much less the same local community, families struggle to find ways to maintain continuity across generations, and in many cases can't hold on to their places.

My father left home at a young age because of an abusive father. He also fled out of economic desperation and the lure of money and more that has steadily pulled people in this country away from rural places. His life path, and those of his brothers and sisters, fits into the story of the "unsettling" described by Wendell Berry in 1979 in *The Unsettling of America*. That story continues today; as a recent United States census reports, less than 2 percent of the American people still make a living off the land.

The personal and historical forces that severed my father's relationship to place ramify into my own life. I am heir to his unsettling, and my imagination and energy for the past several years has focused on healing what I see as the wound of this severing between a person and his or her place. Feeling a lack in my life, I return again and again to the idea that being rooted in a place and in a community will open possibilities of experience impossible to find in a wandering life. For me, the route toward that healing begins with stories.

I want to tell the story of the back room of the shack, the one my father told me about. He said a meteor smashed its roof. He said he almost got killed when that meteor came through late one night. He slept in that corner, he said, and that meteor almost hit him. That's how he told the story. I found out later from an aunt that the roof fell because the support beam rotted, and that it happened years after my dad had already run away to join the air force.

My uncles repaired the roof so they could use the shack as a hunting cabin. They go up to the old place sometimes to get a few deer. Sometimes they go during hunting season, sometimes they go when it's not deer season, but they go when they need meat to make sausage. Uncle Herbert makes the best sausage, but it's really rich, so his sister, Aunt Angie, says she can only eat half a ring before it gives her diarrhea.

I use the back room of the shack as a kitchen. It has a few old school desks and tables, and there's an electric skillet hanging from a nail. Uncle Herbert said he put in electricity a few years ago so there'd be light at night when they hunt. Most nights I cook over a fire, but in the morning I use the skillet to heat water for tea and oatmeal before I work in the garden I've begun here, or start out for a walk.

There's a painting tacked to the wall in the back room of the shack. My grandfather, Opa Ben, made it when the family still lived here. (They called it a home then, not a shack, as Uncle Herbert often reminds me.) Uncle Herbert said: "All I can remember about it is that painting was made there, while we was living there, and it was night, about four in the morning. I woke up and he was painting on that picture. He was working in the light of a coal-oil lamp, and in the morning there was this finished painting."

The painting compels me. A little boy with a cowboy hat on a string hanging behind his neck looks up at a ball he's tossed into the air, and his dog jumps beside him. A stone house with a wooden porch looms in the background. I asked Uncle Herbert if this was a specific house, maybe one where Opa Ben had lived, but Uncle Herbert said it was just something Opa Ben made up in his head. "He would say, I guess, that's how he thought it *should* look. That's what artists do; they don't necessarily see what they're painting, but it's in their mind."

I like this painting because of the layers of nostalgia it's got in it as it hangs there on the wall of the shack's back room. It speaks to me about Opa Ben, a hard man who treated his children and wife badly. He had no joyous early life, yet he had this nostalgic longing for childhood, at least as he imagined it could have been. Aunt Barbara says Opa Ben's childhood wasn't blessed. "He never forgave his sisters—Lucy, Hilda, or Frieda—any of them," Aunt Barbara told me. "He said, 'They did not let me go to school. Oma wouldn't let me go, or any of my sisters.' They said he didn't need the education, and he carried that on into his children."

Then there's the nostalgia Uncle Herbert connects to that painting. Well, not the painting alone, but the story of how he hung it on the wall there. Uncle Herbert bought the old place from my grandmother's "estate" after she died. That is, he and one of his brothers paid a market price for the property, and that money was divided evenly between the other eleven kids. When Uncle Herbert went to clean the place so they could fix the roof, he found the canvas in a trash pile. It was torn from its frame and ragged around the edges, but he nailed it to the wall anyway. He said, "Of course, us kids wrecked everything we had. It's surprising we had the pictures we did have. That one happened to be on a canvas. My father bought the canvas material and bought light wood, and stretched it himself, and put it on himself. It was painted at that house, and it got wrecked up, and when Stephen and I got the house it was laying in some trash pile, and I dug it out, and said, 'Oh, let's put it up there.'" So Uncle Herbert added his layer of nostalgia atop Opa Ben's.

And now I'm adding mine. The painting makes me think all these thoughts about my family now, after my return to them following a long absence. I barely knew Uncle Herbert or Aunt Barbara or my father's other kin because my dad ran away from home when he was only a teenager. As the oldest, he bore the full brunt of Opa Ben's abuse, so he left to join the air force, distancing himself from his brothers and sisters.

The nostalgia I add to this painting connects precisely to all of the stories it brings out of my uncles, my aunts, and me. They tell me Opa Ben did a lot of paintings, and I've seen some of them hanging in the living rooms of various relatives. We had one in our house when I was young—a painting on wood of a deer running in a snowy landscape. It only now strikes me how odd it was that Opa Ben should paint snow, huge piles of it, on the ground. It's odd because Opa Ben spent his entire life in the Texas Hill Country where it rarely snows, and never comes in such piles. "That's what artists do. They don't necessarily see what they're painting, but it's in their mind."

We usually consider nostalgia something to be dismissed. It's just the way some people think "the good old days" had to be better than now. But I wonder whether something more complicated might be going on. Nostalgia comes from two Greek roots, *nostos-*, "to return home," and *algos-*, "pain." Thus, nostalgia literally means, "to return home and suffer pain." In current conventional usage it is a mildly derisive term suggesting a "homesickness" for a past that never existed. People who are nostalgic are thought to be seeking an escape from the complexities of contemporary life by idealizing the past. But there are other etymological memories contained in the word. The Greek root comes out of the Indo-European base **nes-, *nos-*, "to return; to unite," and the etymological dictionaries claim connections for nostalgia in the Gothic *ga-nisan*, "to heal," and *nasjan*, "to save." Old English amplifies with *gi-nesan*, "to survive, be healed." These etymological connections suggest partial explanations for the persistent return of nostalgia in a world where, by some predictions, it should have long ago been eradicated like smallpox. In the contemporary United States, where constant movement leads some people to feel "homeless" even when they have a house, the longing in nostalgia offers both a source of suffering, *algos*, and an attempt to heal that suffering through *nostos*.

I've been thinking about the way the Hill Country seems to be a place of nostalgia. Antique shops dot the roads everywhere. One shop owner told me most of his customers come from Houston, Austin, San Antonio, and Dallas.

The Hill Country town of Fredericksburg—due to its rural, German character—hovers near the top ten in the list of tourist attractions in Texas. Groups from Germany visit every year, and I know of at least two shops on the main street, a bakery and a weaving studio, owned and run by Germans who chose to move to Texas because Fredericksburg felt more *heimlich*, "homelike," than Germany itself. One weekend I walked the main street of town and heard Spanish, Japanese, Danish, and an African language being spoken along with the inevitable English and German.

What kind of nostalgia is this, that it should have such powerful familial, regional, national, and even transnational attraction? I once read that in the late nineteenth century tradition began to replace religion as a moral force. Some have gone so far as to say: "Memory is what we have now in place of religion" (Kammen 1991, 194). This seems interesting to me. It's more than just something clever or ironic or witty to say. It suggests a contemporary longing for connectedness to places, to the stories of places, to the memories embedded in them. Lawrence Goodwyn, in an essay accompanying a set of photographs of the places and people of the Hill Country, wrote:

> A fundamental American dilemma defines itself in the Hill Country today—a kind of dislocation, a confusion about the meaning of the past and our connection to it. This kind of dislocation is not a problem merely for the Germans of the Hill Country but for millions of contemporary Americans as well. It is a problem that many urban newcomers to the Hill Country are trying to escape. With this sense of dislocation comes its corollary, a sense of longing. (Watriss and Baldwin 1991, 39)

It seems this system of nostalgia requires rural or marginalized areas to convey some feeling of richness and fullness for modern urban American culture. Rural places such as the Hill Country and "exotic" cultures like those of Native American peoples become identified as bearers of tradition and rootedness to the earth; and mobile, urban Americans eagerly seek to find a connection, if only briefly and incompletely, by purchasing antiques and "sacred" objects.

The Texas Hill Country has been in my mind since I was a boy. My father moved restlessly during my childhood, dragging his family from one place to another, hoping always to find better work, more money, friendlier folks, a new life. I recall coming into the Hill Country as if it were a foreign land—exotic, full of strange people speaking German, smelling of dry wind and thick cedar brakes, and waking my imagination with its bone-shaped limestones and sparkling rivers. We lived in cities and towns on the urban fringes of the Hill Country—Austin, New Braunfels, San Antonio—but the country remained always the elusive place of intense visits and vivid stories. I spent extended time in the region only after I had grown and set off on my own.

A friend from Houston once told me that the Hill Country is where most Texans would choose to live if they could pick anywhere in the state. If you come from East Texas, my friend told me, you love the feeling of space and openness the region gives. When you rise up out of the humid coastal plain above the Balcones Escarpment, my friend said, you can just feel yourself getting healthier. When you approach the area from the west, the small, well-kept towns remind you civilization does exist in Texas, and the startling sight of spring-fed streams and rivers soaks into you like a cold drink for your parched West Texas soul.

What I found when I moved as an adult to the Hill Country both confirmed and called into question this sense of the place as a home to be desired. Through family and friends, I discovered the stories that tie my past to the land. Through my own wanderings and conversations with the people who live in the region as it is today, I experienced the richness of the place and people and witnessed, disturbingly, a process of flattening that seems to remove the richness of experience, replacing it with a tourist economy lacking depth and local viability. On any given Saturday, you will find thousands of people shopping the streets of Fredericksburg, the town at the center of the region's current economic boom. You can buy anything from dulcimers to decoys, from thousand-dollar antiques and furniture made from African hardwoods to Wild West paraphernalia; but if you look closely at the numbers, you'll find that the town's top business is health care—hospitals and nursing homes employ more people than any other industry. You can be a tourist here, or a retiree, but many of the indicators of a healthy economic culture evolving to meet local needs seem lacking. An organic vegetable farm in the area closed for lack of customers, though you can buy a hundred different flavors of peach preserves in town. Few restaurants that avoid the German menu of sausage and sauerkraut and schnitzel last for any time in town. You can rent a room for a night in one of the area's 300–plus bed and breakfasts, but forget the idea of finding a rental house unless money is no real obstacle. Prices for land that has never been more than marginal for farming and barely adequate for ranching have shot up to $2,000 to $10,000 per acre.

Many books feed the myth and the mystique of the Texas Hill Country as a place. While I've enjoyed reading the stories of pioneers and colorful characters, there always seems to be something missing from these historical accounts and tall tales. I wondered where the experiences of people like my family—the backbreaking and fruitless work and hurtful struggles with poverty—fit with the idyllic tales of harmony with the Indians and steadily improving fortunes of hardworking German families. When I finally met my aunts and uncles on my own terms, as an adult, they introduced me to stories of the Hill Country that I'd neither read nor heard; and despite the hardships, there were stories of joy and living as well as suffering and dying. But they were stories of everyday folks, not folk heroes or victims.

I knew immediately that I wanted to help those stories get told and shared as a counterbalance to the myth, so I began tape-recording my conversations with aunts and uncles. This led me deeper into questioning both what life had been like in the Hill Country in the past and what life is like there now.

My family is not, has never been, one of history's winners. We've gathered no bounty, brought forth no eras. The first Syring in the Hill Country, Christophe Süring, came overland from New Orleans, not with the wave of settlers from Germany. As near as I can reckon based on written sources, he married a New Braunfels widow who had land claims through her husband, and so, through the borrowed "glory" of some other person's pioneering, we came to have our foothold in the hills. It has never been a sure one. A few generations later the Syrings ended up with a marginal ranch of a few hundred acres in Kendall County. It didn't last long. My grandfather's mother left it to an eldest son who ended up a bachelor without children, and the acres of cedar brakes, thin soil, stones, and a stunningly beautiful stretch of cypress-lined creek passed from my family before any of us "made good."

There are no uncles who hit it big, no aunts who married out of their class and "brung us up" in the world. We are a family of meat packers, mechanics, waitresses, data-entry clerks, and truck drivers. If anything, my generation is even further from that elusive American dream of success over generations. Flipping burgers, selling drugs, fixing cars— these are the things we do.

I'm something of an aberration and I know it. I read books. I write. I teach a little. But perhaps I'm not so much of an exception as I think. My family loves language, loves stories. Put three of us in a room and what do we do?

Tell stories, of course.

If you leave us alone in a room long enough, we'll eventually come round to telling stories about the hills. They make us into a group, a family, a community. Whether we've lived there for years or only visited, we feel as though the Hill Country gives us a claim to saying, "I am here. I've lived. I've been a part of the way things are."

This book tells many interconnected stories, but I've divided the stories into sections to give the themes and ideas some shape.

Part 1, "Speaking in Tongues, Telling Tales: Family Stories," introduces the Syring family. As the various conversations I've had with aunts, uncles, and cousins unfold, they evoke the landscapes of experience and stories that compose the collective tale of the Syring family. It is an essayistic grappling with family, home, and particularly, place, as well as my attempts to understand the emotional and intellectual ramifications of trying both to live in a place and to understand the constraints— social, emotional, economic, environmental—of that place.

Part 2, "Honey Creek Church—Chapter and Verse," gathers several short stories focused around a single place to explore how places become containers for memory and story.

Part 3, " Migrations toward Home: Fredericksburg, Texas," includes most of the research I did while living in Fredericksburg, the community at the heart of the Texas Hill Country, and the economic center of the region's current tourist "boom." While I am critical of the use of tourism to revive the town's economy, I do not perform a direct critique of heritage tourism with Fredericksburg as my case study. Instead, I examine some of the problems with creating Fredericksburg as a "home" for German Americans, their descendants, and newcomers to the area. I also highlight some of the regenerative stories of the place that occur despite economic opportunism.

Finally, "Closings: Beginning Again," both closes the circle of my explorations and suggests how the whole process of questioning undertaken here begins over again and again.

Many writers have cited statistics that say one out of four or five people in the United States moves every year. Here, for example, is John Daniels:

> This cottage at the end of the trail, which my wife and I rent, is my twenty-ninth dwelling in forty years—I recalled them the other day while driving I-280 to San Francisco. This is our third summer here. How many more, we can't say—very likely only one or two. . . . I, and millions of others in this country where the average family moves once every four years . . . skim freely from place to place, home to home, reasonably happy and very possessive of our independence, but also just a bit baffled, a bit stifled in our easy movement, sure of what belongs to us but not at all sure of what we belong to. Fluent in mobility, we try haltingly to learn the alphabet of place. (Daniels 1992, 205–206)

My life has been a movement between the Texas Hill Country of my father's family and the Midwest of my mother's family. In the course of such movement, the questions of what family, home, place, and community mean have become complex and crucial for me. In a society as mobile as the United States, such questions loom large.

I don't pretend to know everything or most or even much about what the Hill Country is like, but it seems possible to describe what one person's encounter with the place, people, and problems has been like, and to use that description to unpack a few broader ideas. Texas is such a place of self-mythicizing, always telling larger-than-life stories about what it is as a place. If, as Larry McMurtry observed in the 1970s, the rural, pastoral way of life has passed in Texas, then I must ask: What kind of life has come into being in the rural places and small towns that continue to exist in today's urbanized Texas? What happened to that young boy sitting on the porch? What happened to his children and their children? Are the people of those times still holding place?

The short answer is they're still here, but they've changed a lot.

The long answer is this book, which is part autobiography, part essay, part story collection, and mostly a record of ways of looking at the life of a place.

The Benjamin and Aurelia Syring family, circa 1953. Back row (from left): Nickolaus (author's father), Herbert, Benjamin, Sr., Aurelia, Virginia, Angeline; Front row: Arthur, Benjamin, Jr., Bernadette, Martha.

Big hog ready for butchering, circa 1910–1920.

Part 1

Speaking in Tongues, Telling Tales

FAMILY STORIES

I once told a friend that families were like minefields, that we walk and dance through them never knowing where or when something is going to explode. . . . Next to the image of the minefield, I have . . . added another: family as a living mystery, constantly changing, constantly providing us with clues about who we are, and demanding that we recognize the new and challenging shapes it often takes.

As Mikhail Bakhtin would put it, we are inheritors of a multiplicity of voices and can only think of ourselves as a mixture of, an amalgam of voices, voices that were first shaped in the context of family. While we are encouraged by American culture to think of ourselves as highly singular, we actually experience ourselves in important ways as "essentially affiliated, joined to others and more like them than different from them."

Mary Helen Washington, Introduction to *Memory of Kin*

Notes on a Hog Butchering

I thought I was going to learn a little about dying. I've rarely seen anything die, and have never watched an animal be dressed out for eating. The deer my father brought home when I was a kid were, with a single exception, always already dead. The one time it happened differently, the deer had only been stunned by my father's shot and when he opened the trunk of the car, the deer sprang loose into the yard. Blood was everywhere and I was so terrified that I ducked back into the house and hid while my father or my Uncle Joe got a tire iron out of the car to knock the deer unconscious so they could cut its throat. They hunted the deer out of season, so they had to kill it quietly to prevent the neighbors from hearing and calling the game warden. I never watched them kill a deer, so I thought this trip would be my first lesson in seeing how a big creature dies.

Twenty-five to thirty of us joined in during the weekend (representing only a small portion of the "kingroup" made up of thirteen Syring children with their spouses and children). We slept in my aunt and uncle's battered three-bedroom mobile home, and worked in the butchering barn in the cedar brakes about forty yards away. A solid mass of sleeping bodies covered the floor each morning.

The killing of the hog happened on Thursday night. Only a few of us had arrived by then—Uncle Herbert who owned the place; another uncle, Robert, who lives in Houston; and three of his "sons." Only one of the three boys is his biological son, born from Robert's first marriage to my Aunt Marty. After Aunt Marty and Uncle Robert divorced, Robert began an affair with Aunt Schatze, Marty's sister, causing a minor family scandal that, after Robert and Schatze got married in the Catholic Church, has since become socially irrelevant for the most part. Another of the sons is from Aunt Schatze's first marriage to a man who got the nickname "The Bloodhunter" because he wanted to fight any man who even talked to his wife. The last son belongs to still another aunt, Virginia, who arrived the next day. This teenage boy spent much of his early life being raised by Uncle Robert and Aunt Schatze, because his own parents' marriage ended in divorce, and Aunt Virginia needed help raising her numerous children.

Uncle Herbert's son, Kevin, came for the killing too. Herbert's wife, Aunt Barbara, and their daughter, Dawn, stayed inside the mobile home doing the work that most of the women in my family do first—cooking food for the men to eat after they finish.

Uncle Herbert told his son to get his gun. Kevin returned with a .22 magnum strapped into a leather holster on his hip. He'd just gotten the pistol and holster as partial down payment on an old car he sold to a friend for $400. Kevin appeared very happy to be wearing that pistol. My uncles and cousins passed the pistol around and appreciated it, putting forth various comments about "Dirty Harry." I asked about the difference between a magnum and a regular pistol, whereupon Kevin opened the chamber and handed one of the shells to me. Uncle Robert explained: "See, the shell is longer and has more powder, so it has more power."

Uncle Herbert climbed into the back of the pig trailer. At this point I should describe the animal that was bringing all of this family effort together. She was an old sow who had been, in Uncle Herbert's words, "sucked dry"—which was not entirely accurate I later discovered as I helped remove the skin and found the teats still full of milk. My uncle had bought her the previous day for the low price of $80. Apparently the market for livestock was not particularly good for the seller at the time, but that price made it possible for some family members who couldn't normally afford to pay for the meat to participate.

Uncle Herbert said he usually buys piglets and then feeds them to maturity on his property. He said this guarantees the animals don't get what my uncles call "trichinosis," a disease Uncle Herbert said results from pigs spending too much time in the dirt and mud—something I thought was a logical impossibility given a pig's status as a wallower. This year, however, Uncle Herbert's work for the fire department and as director of Comal County Civil Defense prevented him from taking on the responsibility of daily feedings. And, as I soon learned, the only things Kevin wants to do to pigs is shoot them, and then much later, after the work is finished, eat them.

But here I've digressed from the sow. She was very calm in the back of the trailer, even after my uncle climbed in with her. He told Kevin to give him the gun. He said the bullet must be placed precisely into the pig's tiny brain, which is about the size of a large peach. The bullet doesn't actually kill the animal. After a successful shot to the brain, the pig's jugular is cut open, to "bleed out" the meat, with the action of the heart muscle continuing for a short time after the cut.

While these preparations took place, my uncles and cousins laughed about how Uncle Joe, an uncle who recently moved too far away to come this weekend, "would be doing the shooting if he was here. He likes to do the shooting."

Uncle Herbert held out a sharpened knife saying, "Somebody give this to me fast when I holler for it." I was standing far back, expecting to be appalled by the death, so Uncle Robert took the knife. The sow had turned toward the front of the trailer, and Uncle Herbert talked to her in a low voice: "Come on, you sow"; and Uncle Robert added, "Look over here, bitch."

She finally turned, and Uncle Herbert fired. I flinched a little and cringed, expecting to hear death squeals, but the sow merely jerked her head a bit, grunted once, and remained silent and standing.

Uncle Herbert looked a bit stunned himself. Kevin said, "Don't use the sights, I haven't set them yet." Somebody said, "Boy, if Uncle Joe was here, he'd be jumping all over your ass. He never misses."

Uncle Herbert aimed again and fired to much the same effect. This time everybody started laughing and talking about Uncle Joe, the family marksman. Four more shots emptied the pistol but the pig still stood. I asked: "What's happening? Is he missing?" By this time I had moved much closer, drawn more by astonishment at my uncle's apparent ineptitude than by a desire to be up close at the crucial moment. Uncle Robert said, "No, he's hitting her, but just not in the right place. There's a bunch of bullet holes in her forehead." I looked closely, but couldn't see them, because it was night; the only light was a streetlamp nailed to a cedar post, and I had no idea where I should look or what I should see.

Uncle Herbert gave the gun to his son and said, "Reload it." Kevin went back to the house to get more shells. Uncle Herbert leaned against the inside of the trailer, and the pig stood quietly by. We talked about past years when Uncle Joe or Uncle Herbert shot the pig with the first try. Uncle Robert said, "Face it, old man. You're getting old." Uncle Herbert replied, "My eyes aren't so good anymore."

A pistol shot startled us, and we saw that Kevin had returned around the other side of the trailer, put the gun against the pig's forehead, and shot her. She fell to the floor and her body and legs jerked and thrashed the trailer's side. Uncle Herbert quickly took the knife from Uncle Robert and cut deeply into the underside of the sow's throat. Blood washed across the floor of the trailer. Uncle Herbert had already told me that he wasn't making blood sausage this year, so the loss of the blood went unremarked. The sow had still not made a sound. I asked, "Are they always this quiet?" Uncle Robert said, "Usually they make a lot of noise." The boys provided appropriate squealing sound effects.

Uncle Herbert wasn't satisfied with the rate the blood was flowing; it must come out very quickly because the heart does not pump for long. If too much blood remains in the flesh after the heart stops, the meat's flavor would be different, according to Uncle Robert: not inedible, simply less tasty. Uncle Herbert reached down and put the knife into the wound. He sawed a bit and opened a wider, if somewhat ragged, slash. Soon the blood stopped gushing.

Uncle Herbert climbed out of the trailer. I leaned in to look at the sow's head. Her mouth was open, and her eyes, half-open, half-closed, reflected the image of the streetlamp.

Now we had a dead, three-hundred-pound pig to move from the trailer, remove the guts, and lay out on a makeshift scraping table made of cedar posts bolted to a metal frame.

Uncle Herbert climbed up on the seat of a front-end loader parked nearby and started it. Uncle Robert took a short length of chain and looped it around one of the pig's legs. Uncle Herbert lowered the front of the loader, and Uncle Robert caught the chain on a tooth of the bucket. Uncle Robert said, "My dad used a block and tackle when he did this, and it took a while." Using the loader, they hoisted the sow onto the table in seconds.

My two uncles started working on scraping the hair off the body. Uncle Herbert draped a few old rags over a small portion of the skin and poured boiling water over the rags. He'd had a fifty-five-gallon drum heating over a gas burner all day. The youngest of Uncle Robert's sons, Glenn, crossed back and forth between the table and the drum carrying pitchers of the water. Uncle Robert said, "My dad used to just lower the hog into boiling water. He had this giant drum—bigger than that one, eighty gallons or more—and he'd just lower the hog into it to get the hair loose." I asked, "Why don't you do it that way?" "My dad always just went ahead and rendered the lard. If you do it that way, you start cooking the fat. That's fine if you're going to render the lard, but when you're making sausage you need to leave some of the fat fresh in the meat."

After he soaked the rags with hot water, Uncle Herbert lifted a corner to tug at the hair underneath. When it came off with little effort, he said: "It's ready," and Uncle Robert started scraping with a small cleaver blade that had a broken handle. The hair came off easily, and after a few scrapes a bald spot marked the pig's shank where the skin was very white and smooth. It looked like a monk's tonsure.

Uncle Robert kept scraping, and though nobody ordered me to, I picked up another cleaver and started on the next spot Uncle Herbert indicated. When we got a good amount of the first side scraped bare, Uncle Robert said, "If Joe was here he'd be slapping her." His hand came down with a loud smack as a demonstration. "I don't know why, but he likes to slap them while he's scraping."

After we scraped both sides of the hog clean of hair, Uncle Herbert climbed onto the front-end loader, and raised the body to be gutted. Uncle Herbert came around the front and began an incision from the pig's anus downward, but somebody called him from the trailer for a phone call. Uncle Robert took over. The dim lighting made it hard to see what he did, but soon he had the pig's abdomen open down to the ribs. Uncle Robert held onto the internal organs with one hand and cut with the other. He took out a few organs—the liver and heart—and gave them to Glenn to set aside for later. "What you're supposed to do is keep the stomach to cook the *pannis* in," Uncle Robert said. "We did it that way a couple of times, but it's easier to just cook it in a big pot."

He kept cutting, but something went wrong. "Son of a bitch!" he said. Liquid ran out of the body cavity onto the ground. "What happened?" I asked. "I cut the piss sack." "Will that ruin the meat?" "No, it just makes it harder to work in here." The lower part of the cavity filled with liquid, but he kept working to get the body cleaned out.

When he finished he rinsed the blood and urine out with a hose, and the hog hung, stripped of hair and organs, pale blue in the lamplight.

NOTEBOOK FRAGMENT

My kin were following their own aesthetic, laboring over the body of a hog stripped of hair. I had my fingers in the milkfat still dripping with milk & I was making tentative cuts with my knife. I was calm, or I wasn't. I felt like my fingers were plunged into a bucket of saliva & my hands were waiting there for something (but I can't think of what). This laboring toward an aesthetic, what was it teaching me? When I find it, I'll know whether it can be written.

Everything under these cedar trees is stone.
My father brought me here. I refused to watch
while he hunted deer in the headlights.
I first drank water from Curry Creek
the night he claimed sixteen for his freezer.

We sat late around a kitchen table. They talked
about the meat, what to do with it.
"We'll make sausage," my father said.

You can't make sausage like I do.
Nobody can.
Not every piece of meat seasons the same.
You can't cure it right.
You don't know the things I do.
I've been blessed—a pinpoint tongue.
I taste everything, the seasonings.
I make the best sausage:
I've got the tongue for it.
The most flavorful meat's right here—
here where the arteries spread from the heart.
The best meat's where there's the most blood.
Uncle Alfred taught me that. Uncle Alfred,
Uncle Falteen, Grandpa Scheel, those men knew
what they were doing when it came to butchering.
They taught me.

My father, talking about sausage, alone,
as if he had made everything—the deer, the hog
and the life that goes into the making.

Feeling for the Bones

"You have to just sort of do it by touch," Aunt Schatze says. Her hands
are greasy with boiled pork, and she rubs meat through the tips of her
fingers. Aunt Virginia and Aunt Angie both nod as they work their
fingers the same way. Their faces are stark under the bare light in the
butcher shed; lines and creases stand out, shadowed rivers of concern
and concentration.

I've got my own hands in a bowl of the same cooked meat. I've been trying to see the tiny fragments that have cooked off the skull and other bones, but my aunts all point out that you can't always see the bones, you have to feel for them.

Last night, after we scraped the hog clean of hair, the men left it hanging to cool. Today we all pitched in to cut the meat from the bones so that tomorrow we can mix it, grind it, and stuff sausage casings. As we cleaned the meat off each section of the hog's skeleton, we threw the bones into a huge cauldron of boiling water to cook off the remnants of fat and flesh and marrow. Tonight, while the men talk inside and eat supper, Aunt Schatze, Aunt Virginia, and Aunt Angie, who came late this afternoon, gather around the big processing table in the butcher shed to feel their way through the leavings from the pot. We are preparing to make *pannis*. We'll mix the shreds of meat with cornmeal, salt, and spices, then cook it down in the big cauldron. Afterward we'll package up "bricks" and put them into freezers to be used later—sliced into patties and fried.

My aunts talk while they work, catching up on family news and explaining things to me. Because my father and mother moved around a lot, I'm mostly ignorant of the complex web of relationships between the several hundred people that make up the extended Syring kingroup.

Aunt Angie and I take a break and go out to sit under a live oak where we look up at the stars and talk quietly. She's explaining what happened when her youngest son, Paul, was born with a birth defect.

"They had to make an opening for him to eliminate waste, he had no muscle there," she says. Paul is a year younger than I. "He nearly died."

We've gotten into a conversation about physical problems, a topic of some recent concern since two of my aunts—Barbara and Jean—are currently battling breast cancer. Uncle Herbert is struggling with an old shoulder injury aggravated by a fall while working as a firefighter. Uncle Jerry, on disability for more than a year, injured himself at his job as a diesel mechanic. He was lifting a heavy tire and twisted his back. He will never again be able to return to normal physical activity, and is seeking an insurance settlement that will provide him with enough money to set up a business as a musician and disc jockey for parties. Before the accident, he had lost the extra weight that plagues many members of my family, but since his injury, he has grown nearly as overweight as his father had been. His body has become a walking memory of the large man who used to make the children rub his legs at night because they were sore from a day of holding up all that weight.

The conversation continues and expands into the past when we go back inside. I ask a question and Aunt Barbara says, "Your grandfather expected the kids to stay home until they were 21 years old, and they were to give every cent they earned at a job to him. And if he felt maybe that he wanted to give them some, he would give them some. Most of the time he did not."

"The specific memories that I have of seeing Opa Ben are things that sort of confirm his role as a patriarch," I say. "Like visiting them in New Braunfels and sitting down to dinner—this was while the youngest of his kids were still living at home—and we'd sit down to eat, and they'd be sitting on that bench along the wall, you know, and he'd be sitting at the head of the table. The kids would all be eating brown beans, and he'd be eating a steak or a roast or something."

"Herb has said a lot of times that Opa Ben would get the best food, and then the kids would get whatever was left—the fat off the brisket or something. I think Ben felt he needed the food because he claimed he was doing the major part of the work; this was not necessarily true. The surgery Herb recently had on his shoulder, part of it is due to his father making them carry the cedar posts they carried—ten- and twelve-foot cedar posts that were a foot around. That started tearing the ligaments in his shoulders, cutting them. It's taken forty or so years, thirty years, for it to catch up with him, but Herb's shoulder problems started back then."

"You think the rest of his body had to sort of break down, and then the old wound manifested?"

"Yeah, it just kept breaking down. And when he fell at the fire station, it finished it off."

"So that was how they made their living for a while, cutting cedar posts?"

"Well, they'd also build fence. Your grandfather always wanted to have his own business. He didn't go to World War II because he worked in the Frederick plant, the refrigeration plant in San Antonio, which was declared vital to the war effort. So he didn't go to war. Besides, he had a bunch of kids. He always wanted to have a business of his own. And they raised baby chicks, hatched baby chicks for a while. They charcoaled for a while, and there's some lot of stories with the charcoal kilns."

"Really? I've never heard any of those."

"Oh yeah. Then they'd build fence. That's how Opa lost his eye."

"That's right! I remember now that he had a bad eye."

"He was stretching barbed wire, and the wire broke and it flew back and hit him in the eye. But it didn't take the whole eyeball, just the vision. He lost enough out of the eye to lose his sight."

"I remember it being glazed over or something. It looked glassy, and always looked toward one direction."

"Well he couldn't do anything with it; it was just blind."

My other aunts—Angie, Schatze, Virginia—have been talking together about other things while Barbara and I talk. I find myself looking at these women's massive bones. I look down at my own long body that friends have sometimes described as gaunt, and remember my mother's joke about me being the milkman's son. My father, my grandfather, my uncles and aunts, my cousins, even the boy in the painting tacked to the wall of the shack—all have big bones and solid muscles. The imaginary boy in the painting has more claim to being part of this family than I do. But these women telling stories, these men teaching me how to do this work, they don't need to see the resemblances to weave me into this fabric of kin. This afternoon one of my cousins went around asking everybody when their birthdays are. Mine happens to be tomorrow, and when this came out, Aunt Angie led everybody into songs for me—"Happy Birthday," "For He's a Jolly Good Fellow." Sometimes you can't see the bones, you have to feel for them.

Resting in the Spirit

Aunt Barbara. How to write about this aunt that I met for what could really be called the first time only recently. My father has been estranged from his family for some years, and I have been even further estranged from him for some years as well, so I only knew her marginally when I was very young.

Barbara's a healer. She says she has the gift of healing. Also the gift of visions. She has sat on the porch of her mobile home and seen the Vision of the Dancing Sun. In moments of quiet and meditative prayer, Aunt Barbara sees the sun dancing in the sky, in front of the clouds, dazzling her eyes with light and color, especially blue, which she says is Mary's color.

Aunt Barbara. "She's not a healthy woman"—a friend said this to me after meeting her for the first time. While she was under anaesthetic for surgery, the doctors found cancer in her uterus and performed a hysterectomy. "Performed" seems such a strange verb—was she suppose to applaud their quick hands moving inside her unconscious body? They also found breast cancer, and weeks later performed a mastectomy and immediate reconstructive surgery with a silicon insert. Should she take back her applause at their clever construction games now that such inserts have been recalled like defective cars from an assembly line because they tend to spring potentially harmful leaks of silicon inside women's bodies?

Aunt Barbara, the healer, is ill, recovering from illness. When she goes to the charismatic Catholic service in San Antonio, her hands grow warm while she watches the healing team treat people with their hands and words. She used to be a member of the healing team, but her cancer has kept her from making the eighty-mile round-trip every Thursday night. My friend and I went with her one Thursday, and Aunt Barbara, feeling the heat rise in her palms, wanted to help heal, but felt reluctant to participate because she had been gone so long. She held her hands in the air, directing her palms toward a healer praying over and touching a middle-aged woman who said she had cancer. My friend encouraged her, and Aunt Barbara walked around the steps to assist the healer praying to the right of the altar. Aunt Barbara stood behind the woman and held her open palms a few inches from the woman's back. The healer nodded to Aunt Barbara and continued speaking to the woman seeking healing. Soon the woman lay back into Aunt Barbara's hands and she lowered her gently to the floor. She told me later: "They used to call it 'slain in the Spirit' but I guess that didn't sound right. Now we call it 'resting in the Spirit.'"

Aunt Barbara helped the healer with many more people, praying quietly to herself and floating her open palms over their backs. All around us, people talked quietly in pews or stood around watching the four chief healers work. When the line of people seeking prayer and healing stopped, the healer whom Aunt Barbara was helping shook her hand and asked how she had been. He asked whether she would like a healing prayer for herself, and she nodded. He began praying. She lay back in his arms, falling in the Spirit.

Aunt Barbara's visions don't come from the distant mystic, the retreat of the hermitage, or the university. They are there in the walk of the everyday. Because she is a woman in a family that has always required her to work hard, either in the household or at a job, her visions have had to be part of the everyday world. There has been no time or leisure for extended solitary meditation. She rides through the Hill Country in the back of her step-father's car and the Dancing Sun is there. She used to drive a school bus, and she meditated and prayed on the way to her first stop, turning the wheel with one hand and counting the rosary with the other between the shifting of gears.

When I visit her at the trailer where she lives with Uncle Herbert we talk about her visions.

"Oh, this was a wonderful time," she says while looking at her journal, which lay open before us on the kitchen table. "This was March. This is August. There was a prayer novena going on in San Antonio. Nine days of prayer. And that was just fantastic."

"So you went down there every day for . . . "

"For nine days," she says.

"I see you write your journal to . . . it says, 'Dear Lord.' That's how you write your journal?"

"Yeah. It's like a letter I'm writing to him. Then I can . . . pour everything out. And sometimes I close it just with an 'amen.' And 'Praise the Lord.' And sometimes I don't. It's just a thank you. It depends on how it goes that day," she says while flipping through the pages. "And I was . . . It was super fantastic and I could see the miracle of the Dancing Sun."

"The Dancing Sun? What is that?"

"Look directly at the sun and it spins this way. And it spins this way. And it bounces exactly like that, and it bounces in the sign of the cross. And there's beautiful colors coming off it."

"You saw this?"

"Um-huhm. And it appears to be coming closer to earth. As a matter of fact, I've seen it when it looks like it's on *this* side of the clouds. There are clouds behind it. But, you don't just look at it. You've got to pray for the grace . . . to be in the state of grace to see it. And then, when you first glance up there'll be, like a cross—some people see a cross, I've seen . . . usually what I see is just a brilliant shaft of light that's a cross. Some people see a wooden cross. Some people see a silhouette of Jesus. And then there's a disk that slides in front of the sun. Okay. It's like, the majesty and glory of God is behind it, and Jesus is in front of it, in front of Him, so that you can see it, and it doesn't hurt your eyes."

"How long does something like this last? When you see something like this are you aware of the passage of time?"

"Sometimes yes, and sometimes no."

"So you've seen this more than once?"

"Um-huhm. I've seen it here. I've seen it just driving down the road, when I've been in prayer. In a state of grace. I drove with mom and Steve down to Nixon, to the property down there, and it's a . . . heck to be with my stepfather sometimes. And we were coming back up Purgatory Road, and the sun was coming in from the west in the evening, you know, it was really bright and blinding. And I was praying, and I looked up and saw the disk go in front of the sun. And then the colors were just fantastic. And the whole area changed different colors. To blue. To red. To gold and yellow and green."

"So the disk is . . . the Host?"

"The Host . . . yeah . . . it's Jesus that we see in the mass, the Host. And it takes some of the intensity off of God the Father so that we might see some of His brilliance. Then there are lights that come off the back side of the Host, behind it, and that's just gorgeous. Then you see, like, disks coming down, and they say that's Mary's rosary beads."

"Around the sun?"

"Yeah. They'll be just like balls."

"Are they disks of light?"

"They're disks of color. Um-huhm. Sometimes they're blue, sometimes they're gold. A lot of times they're blue. Mary's color is blue. One time I was praying and I noticed the Miracle of the Dancing Sun was happening, and this was right out here. And then I held the camera directly into the sun." She hands me a photograph. "I don't know what I did with that other picture."

"Describe to me . . . I mean, I see this as simply being a very beautiful sunset. Describe to me what you're seeing here."

"This . . . the gold is the majesty of the Lord. And on this one, doesn't it appear that the sun is almost on this side of the trees?"

"Um-huhm."

"And those are the trees right out here across the road."

"Was this in the morning or the evening?"

"This was in the evening sunset. I had been saying the rosary, and I really hadn't thought about too much, but when the Host goes in front of the sun, the light depth changes. And that's how I knew the miracle was happening for me. And it's a much softer light. And when the miracle of the sun was happening, it would just slowly drift, the whole unit, like a piece of cloth drifting to the ground. And it would be in different colors. It would be in red, for the blood and mercy of Jesus. It would be in gold, for his majesty, for God's majesty. It would be in blue, for Mary's blue. In green, for healing. The different shades of green. And usually when I . . . I have visions, that's been one of my gifts, is visions . . . and when I see visions, I see just the heart of Jesus sometimes, just his heart. And then it's in imperial pinks and blues. It's not a real red color. Almost a chartreuse color, almost a hot pink color, only not quite.

"Just the heart?"

"Just the heart, then that's the color that's behind it. And I see that in my mind. In my mind's eye."

"When does that come?"

"In prayer usually."

"You said you were just sitting and being quiet?"

"Yeah. I was praying the rosary."

"You were praying the rosary. Were you doing it outside?"

"Yeah, I was sitting out here on the porch praying the rosary."

"So you like to pray outside?"

"Sometimes, yeah. The kids were hounding me to no end, and so I went outside to say a rosary."

"So sometimes at moments of quiet and prayer, you have these visions?"

"Yeah."

Storyteller

Uncle Herbert's hands, that's what comes first. They're huge, thick, like stone. If he made a fist, it would be a boulder. All the Syrings have hands like that, my father too. Herbert isn't an old man, but his sight is already fading. When he needs to read something, he cocks his head so he can look at the words through bifocals—it's a strangely vulnerable gesture for such a big man.

Uncle Herbert and Aunt Barbara are both storytellers. When I visit them at their mobile home in the Hill Country a pattern has developed.

I drive down from Houston in the afternoon and spend the evening drinking iced tea and talking with Aunt Barbara while Uncle Herbert works late as a security guard at Yellow Rock, a country-and-western dance hall, or works an all-night shift at the New Braunfels Fire Department. In the morning we wake early when Uncle Herbert comes home. We sit at the cluttered table and drink coffee. We eat homemade sausage or bacon and *pannis* and tell stories. When I suggest that Uncle Herbert is the "memory keeper" of the family, he agrees, and gives me a story.

"Well, Arthur, me, and Ben, when we was living up there [at the shack], went out venturing, and we were big thieves, at least we thought we were. And right down the road—I don't know if it's still there, it might still be there—was a hunter's cabin. Herbst's hunter's. So we went down, we broke in that house. Back in the fifties. They had a nice little portable radio. We stole that. We stole a fifth of Seagram's Seven. And I can remember the song that was playing when we turned it on was "Pick Me Up on Your Way Down." Right then that was real popular. And we got out there a ways and listened to this radio about half an hour, and we said, "No. We stole too much, we need to put the radio back." [laughs] So we broke back into the house, and put the radio back. But we kept the fifth of whiskey since there were other bottles around there."

"You didn't think they'd notice it was missing?"

"We were like Kevin [Herbert's own son] when he said that white van came and pulled the washline down. When Kevin was a few years old, he was hanging on the washline in the back yard, and he broke it. He tried to get out of it by telling a story about a white van. He said some white van came driving through the back yard and drove right through that clothesline. He was justifying it. So we'd take something up to Daddy and say 'I found it, so it's mine.' That's why, when Kevin wondered how I knew he was lying, that's how I knew it, because we also pulled that stuff. Except I didn't take it home to Daddy."

"No, you usually took it to Mama, and Mama didn't know any better," Aunt Barbara interrupts. "She had no idea that you would do such a thing."

"So we took that bottle up toward the house," Uncle Herbert continues. "And then we all had, oh, four or five good hits on it, and then we buried it out in the pasture in a couple trees, and every chance we got, we took a hit on it. And it was almost full at one time, and it was working its way down, even long after we moved away from there it was still in that brushline. And Ben or I or Arthur when we'd go up there, we'd go down to those trees and tap it, and take two or three good shots. One time when I went up there, and we hadn't been up there for years, I went looking for it and couldn't find it. Then I found it, and it was already moved by the animals or something, and it was laying in another location, had no label left on it, nothing. And all it had was a third or so left. So I just picked the bottle up, and we still got it. That bottle, it's sure mellow. It's . . . well it was in '58 when we swiped it out of the hunter's camp, and I guess we could always take it back and give it back to them, what's left of it. The big thieves," he concludes while laughing.

"So now you guys drink it just when you're all three together?"

"One time we had all of us here, so we all took a little nip. Memories."

Hunter's Raid

It started as a simple enough venture. Herbst's hunter's cabin sat well back in the hills, away from any roads, and it would be empty this time of year—groups from places as far away as Houston and Dallas visited the place during deer season, but the only use it got the rest of the time was as a shelter for mice and snakes.

Herbert was the one who came up with the idea to hide down by the creek until after the school bus picked up the younger kids. Then he thought the three of them could go fishing down on the river, but Arthur had a different idea.

"If we're going to risk getting our asses beat, we might as well do something special stead of just hitting the same old fishing holes."

He suggested they go over to the Herbst place to see what there was to see, and maybe what there was to steal. Herbert had nothing against such a plan; he was always willing to venture what his younger brother suggested, and young Ben kept his mouth shut most of the time.

The three of them walked downstream from the low-water crossing and hid behind the giant cypress there while the bus pulled up, opened its mouth, and swallowed their younger brothers and sisters. Skipping school had become such a habit for the three boys that the other children didn't mention it to Annie or their father unless they had a particular grievance against one of the three. Even then, the decision whether to tell or not had to be weighed carefully because telling on one meant all three got a whipping, and then the other two would get their own revenge on whoever tattled.

Besides, the school principal had stopped worrying about Süring absences ever since he'd driven out to the country place to be met by Ben Sr. with a belt in his hand and hard words in his mouth.

"Your oldest boy, Nicklaus, has been missing a lot of days, Mr. Süring," the principal had said from outside the gate of the place. "Wonder if we might talk some."

Ben Sr. had been pulling his belt on through the loops at his waist, but now he pulled it out and let its forty-eight inches dangle down from his hand and drag in the dry grass outside the shack he lived in.

"My kids come to school when they can," he said. "Sometimes I got more necessary things for them to do. Then they don't come to school."

"Well, that's fine, Mr. Süring," the principal said. "But the state says those children are supposed to have a certain number of days of schooling each year. You don't want the children to come up uneducated do you?" He put his hand on the gate to let himself inside the tight barbed-wire fencing surrounding the place.

"Mister," Ben Sr. said slowly, "You ain't about to open that gate. This my property. Them my children. When I need them, they won't be coming to school, and for your 'education,' it don't take knowing too many books to stretch a fence or mind a *kohlehaver*, which is what this family does, now does it?"

The principal stood there with his hand resting on the wire and looked at the fat man with the belt. Ben Süring's bones were massive, and when his fingers were closed like that around the leather of the belt, his hands resembled huge, knuckly limestones more than a man's hands. The principal wasn't a small man, but he could tell Ben Süring outweighed him by more than a hundred pounds.

"Well I certainly am sorry to hear you're so recalcitrant, Mr. Süring." He dropped his hand from the fence wire. "I suppose I could take your words right now as a threat of violence against me, but frankly I've got better things to do than waste my energies in a philosophical disagreement with a hillbilly over the values of schooling to give his children something more than he apparently was given." He turned away from the gate, and began climbing back into his car. "You're a man in a difficult spot," he said as he slammed shut the door. "But you're also a damn fool."

Ben had slowly drawn on his belt while the principal backed around and drove off toward the county road.

So Herbert, Arthur, and Ben Jr. felt relatively secure in their truancy.

They spent much of the morning following the bends of the creek upstream, not even bothering to duck into the cedar brakes when they happened on Walter Wendenworth putting in a new stretch of fence to keep his sheep from wading the creek and mixing with the Kneiper livestock on the other side. Herbert and Arthur stopped to help the old man stretch the wire taut while Ben Jr. waded into the creek and tried to catch minnows with his hands.

"Your father's eye heal up yet?" Wendenworth asked when they finished.

"It's gone dead," Herbert answered. "Ain't never going to heal up now."

"Might could happen to anybody trying to restretch old wire. Still just the same, Lord knows Ben don't need another hindrance from making a living. He going to keep stretching when it gets well enough to work again?"

"Already doing it," Herbert said. "Went over to San Antonio today to get a new come-along. He says he don't trust the old one anymore."

"Got bad luck in it," Wendenworth nodded. "Thanks for the help here, now. Would a took me all day if you hadn't pitched in."

The three of them turned when Ben Jr. started yelling and splashing as he quickly climbed out of the creek.

"What's going on?" Arthur yelled. "You having a fit or something?"

Ben Jr. ran over to them, panting and chattering.

"I saw a gar. A big one! Must a been seven, eight feet. Almost bit my hand off."

Wendenworth started laughing.

"Ain't any gar in that little creek big enough to do you harm, not when it's so low. The big ones probably don't even come up the creek from the river this time a year."

The four of them walked over to the creek and looked down into the clear water. Below the pool, where the water ran shallow and swift, a long, thick stick had caught up on the stones.

"There's your big gar," Arthur said, picking up the stick and brandishing it at Ben Jr. "Watch out, he might eat your nose!"

The three of them laughed while Ben Jr. shrugged.

By the time they got to the draw where the hunting cabin sat it was past noon. Arthur decided to make the whole thing an assault, and they lay down on their bellies in the dry dirt and crawled on their elbows under the cedar scrub surrounding the cabin.

The cabin was old and well made, the walls built up out of limestone, the roof recently redone with new sheet metal. It was long, like a barracks, and had several windows set in on all sides. They approached it from behind and could see the screened sleeping porch, which was full of folded and stacked cots.

"You go round that way." Arthur whispered to Herbert and pointed to the right. "I'll circle left and come up from this side."

"What I'm going to do?" Ben Jr. asked.

"Stay here. Make sure nobody don't come running through that back door and take off to get help."

Ben Jr. didn't want to stay put, but he agreed because he knew he was fortunate that he'd been given a role to play at all. The two older boys started in their respective directions, still crawling on their elbows through the dry cedar needles covering the ground. Herbert scraped an arm and cursed out loud, but Arthur told him to keep quiet and not complain about wounds taken in action. Soon they had worked their way around to the front of the cabin. Arthur examined the wooden door from a distance; it was as well made as the rest of the building and sat snugly in its frame. There was no gap at the bottom.

"Probably it's locked up tight," Arthur called. "We'll have to break a window or something to get inside."

Herbert had nothing against breaking things. He was always helping Nicklaus, their oldest brother, to shoot out the glass that their father tried to keep in their own windows at the shack, but Herbert didn't think breaking a window here was a good idea.

"They'll figure it was us, and tell Daddy," he reasoned. "Any time something gets broke round here, people figure it was one a us. We got to do this so it looks like a professional job, so they think some thief from somewhere else came along and did it."

The two of them lay watching the door for a few minutes and thinking. Arthur agreed with his brother's reasoning, but didn't have any other ideas on how to proceed and was about to break a window anyway when the door started to open. Their hearts started pounding hard—they had treated the secrecy as a game, but now quickly crawled backward a bit to hide in the cedar shade. The door swung wide open, and Ben Jr.'s face came out into the sunlight. He was laughing.

"I got them from behind," he giggled. "They weren't expecting an ambush."

He had gotten tired of waiting in the dirt and approached the cabin from behind. The door to the sleeping porch hadn't been locked, and the cabin's back door was propped open by a folded cot.

They went inside, Arthur leading the way. The door opened into a room dominated by a large table surrounded by rush-bottom chairs. On the open shelves they could see bottles, though there wasn't enough light inside to make out the labels.

"Prop the door open with a chair," Arthur ordered, and Herbert did so.

With the added light, they could see that most of the bottles were without labels and full of clear liquid. None of them had any experience with alcohol. Ben Sr. had been a famous drunk when they lived over behind the church, famous because he had suprisingly been a sweet drunk, mellowing as the liquor loosened him up rather than growing mean and violent. He would drink wine and play his fiddle, and suddenly there would be a jovial fat man sitting there singing where a short time before there had only been pig-headed Ben Süring scowling at anybody who looked sideways. But when a doctor down in New Braunfels told Ben Sr. that his liver was defective and he would die within five years if he didn't stop drinking altogether, alcohol became a forbidden presence in his household. Arthur opened one of the unmarked bottles and smelled it. He couldn't tell whether it was medicinal, alcoholic, or something else.

"Could be water in an old bottle. Could be moonshine. Could be poison," he proclaimed, offering the bottle to Ben Jr. "You were the one who broke through their defenses, you try a little first."

"I may be younger than you, but that don't mean I'm dirt dumb. I'm not drinking anything less I know what it is first. You drink it."

Nobody had the courage to give it a try. Herbert wandered over to the table while Arthur rummaged farther back in the cabinets. On a window sill behind the table Herbert found a transistor radio. He turned it on and set the volume loud, and soon Patsy Cline's voice drowned out the noise Arthur made knocking the bottles together.

"Found one!" Arthur held up a bottle that still had a label on it, and whose top had never been opened. He pulled the cap off and smelled it.

"Seagram's Seven," he said and took a short sip, and for the first time felt the same fire that used to forge his father into a music man.

Herbert left the radio playing and took the bottle from his brother for a deep swig that brought him up coughing.

"Seems like it might be poison after all," he sputtered and handed the whiskey to Ben Jr.

"Daddy's going to kill us if he smells this stuff on us," Ben Jr. said while looking warily at the bottle in his hand.

"He won't know. He comes home late tonight," Herbert said. "He's going to stop at the farmer's market after it closes to see about getting some cheap melons. We'll be in bed by the time he comes."

Ben Jr. nodded and took his own first sip. His face crumpled, but he said nothing.

"Take that," Herbert said and pointed to the radio. He recapped the whiskey and headed toward the back door. "And put that board back across the front door."

They went down to the creek and splashed downstream a ways before they stopped to take a few more sips, feeling giddy as much with the terror of being found out as with the alcohol. The sun was hot now, and they decided to swim for a while in the deep hole they called the "Blau Kumbe," the place with a gravel bar beside it, diving from the shallow to the deep with the KSHOOM sound of bodies meeting water.

Other Voices: Toni Morrison

If writing is thinking and discovery and selection and order and meaning, it is also awe and reverence and mystery and magic. I suppose I could dispense with the last four if I were not so deadly serious about fidelity to the milieu out of which I write and in which my ancestors actually lived. Infidelity to that milieu—the absence of the interior life, the deliberate excising of it from the records that the slaves themselves told—is precisely the problem in the discourse that proceeded without us. How I gain access to that interior life is what drives me and is part of this talk which both distinguishes my fiction from autobiographical strategies and which also embraces certain autobiographical strategies. It's a kind of literary archaeology: on the basis of some information and a little bit of guesswork you journey to a site to see what remains were left behind and to reconstruct the world that these remains imply. What makes it fiction is the nature of the imaginative act: my reliance on the image—on the remains—in addition to recollection, to yield up a kind of truth.

"The Site of Memory," in *Inventing the Truth:*
The Art and Craft of Memoir

Material Remains

When Opa Ben died, my grandma had arranged for some of his things to be sold through a closed-bid auction. She kept the things she wanted, then offered what remained to the children.

The entries in the written record of the auction look like this:

Item	Condition	Price
1957 Chevy pickup	poor	350.00
belt-sander	good	50.00
paint-brushes	fair	.50

At the bottom of each page is a hand-written note:

"I, Aurelia Syring, Reserve the Right to Reject Any or All Bids."

And at the end of the list is a longer note of explanation:

Dear Sons & Daug's

Here is a List of Items that I would like to sell. You'll have first chance to buy.

The fair market value reflects what I think is a fair price now. Conditions are what the equipment is in now. There are no guarantees, so an on site inspection is suggested.

All SEALED BIDS are due at my home at 290 Highway 81 W. New Braunfels, TX 78130 at 2:00 pm on Sunday 7th day of March 1982. Each party will have 90 Calendar Days to pay in cash and before picking up their Items. Any Items Left after that date I will not be responsible for.

I will Reserve all rights to reject any or all Bids.

All wood products of Father will be given to each by a number system, that I will be using myself.

Your fair consideration will be appreciated.

Your Loving Mother,
Aurelia Syring

Despite the signature, it seems an oddly impersonal document, and in some ways, it has become an archaeological site, a clue for my attempt to understand who Oma Relia might have been. Mostly I remember a fallen-shouldered woman who always had her hair pulled up in a net and who lived uneasily in a body slowed to old age by the time she was in her fifties. When Aurelia, my father's mother, died, I was living with my other grandma in Nebraska, so I didn't go to the funeral.

I'm not sure whether Oma Relia realized she was setting a precedent for her own material remains, but when she died, her things were auctioned to her children using an even more elaborate system. This time, however, the auction was live—that is, most of the children drove out to Uncle Herbert's place to attend. On the way down from Austin to attend both the funeral and the auction my father hit a deer and nearly added himself, my mother, and my two youngest sisters to those who were to be mourned rather than those who were to mourn. That experience—the death of his mother and the near death of himself and his own family—continues to have repercussions in my father's life. He has been a "born-again" Christian ever since nearly dying in that accident.

The list of things my grandmother had in her possession when she died runs to six hundred items, but this hardly indicates wealth in economic terms. The total estimated "market" worth of these six hundred things is $3,380, a generous number arrived at by Uncle Herbert who was executor of the will. The list has been neatly copied from the original rough form used at the auction onto large sheets of fourteen-column ledger paper. One of my cousins copied the list, along with the bid amounts by each of the thirteen children, onto the ledger paper because Uncle Herbert wants to preserve the list for future reference and remembrance. Fragments of the family's past and Oma Aurelia's everyday life are evoked by items listed on those pages. An excerpt from the list includes the following:

1-13	Food in jars (9)	1.00
2-23	3 old Quilts	10.00
2-46	Cross	.50
2-47	Cross	.50
2-48	Cross	.50
2-49	Cross	.50
2-50	Cutting Board	2.00
3-22	Last Supper Puzzle	.10
3-23	Queen size panty hose	.10
3-48	One arm broken rocker	.25
4-22	Wood Deer	5.00
4-23	Wood Lion	5.00
4-24	Wood Large Roadrunner	.50
4-25	Wood Rooster	3.00
4-26	Wood Sm. Roadrunner	2.00
4-27	Wood Sm. Roadrunner	2.00
4-28	Wood Sm. Roadrunner	2.00
4-41	Violin Strings	.25
4-49	40th Wedding Anniv. Vase	.25

It is a remarkable document, containing the material outlines of the stories of this woman's interior life. Some of the items seem to be oddities—"5-4 3 vases taped together 1.00"—while other objects in the list combine to tell simple stories that look like the equations of a life.

I can read, for example, the story of one period of my grandmother's life in the following entries: "5-34 5 small aprons + 5-35 2 red chef aprons + 5-36 7 chef aprons + 5-37 2 red white aprons." What does this life equation equal? Oma Aurelia worked for a number of years in New Braunfels as a cook in an "icehouse" restaurant. During the week she stayed in a rental room in town—perhaps the only time in her life that she ever had a "place" of her own.

Those crosses, that Last Supper puzzle, and many other religious items echo my grandmother's year as a young woman living in a convent in San Antonio. Eventually she took a job as a domestic for an older couple, but according to my aunts and uncles, that job ended under a cloud of disgrace—some scandal about which I can gather only fragments. Based on the stories, I think Oma Aurelia was raped by the man who employed her. My grandfather must have made the typical move of "blaming the victim" because my aunts remember that Opa Ben often said to Oma Aurelia that she was lucky he had accepted her, even despite her disgrace.

Oma Aurelia came from a genetic heritage of solid German women, but life was not kind to this woman who gave birth to fourteen children in less than twenty years. I showed a friend two photographs of Oma Aurelia—one taken just before she got married, and one years later after the births of her children. My friend commented that not only was she older and more tired in the later photograph, she looked like two entirely different women who might have been related, but hardly closer in family resemblance than distant cousins.

Talking about Dresses

She was a rag woman.

My mother had more new dresses that hung in the closet that she never wore, because she was a rag woman. She wore these old clothes all the time. And she had beautiful clothes in her closet—even a couple of dresses that hadn't ever been worn more than once. She just didn't feel comfortable dressed up. Washed-out clothes is what she wore. All the way to her death she was wearing those old things.

They should have buried her in that same old housedress she was wearing when she died. She knew all along they would put her body into that dress we'd all bought for her to wear to the fortieth anniversary party, and they would put her in the ground next to where my father was in the suit we'd bought for him to wear that day, too.

Not too long before my mama died, I sat down on the bed once and looked at the dresses hanging in her closet. Looking at her dresses was like remembering. The gray one with piping I remembered. It was covered in plastic, so I tore a little corner of the wrapping to feel the fabric.

It was cold. She had worn that dress once, the day they'd buried Lucy Price. Aunt Lucy was a big woman with a tongue like water, smooth talking and ready to tell a story if it meant a person might listen. The morning they put Lucy Price down had been cold. I felt that cold just as sure as my mama had when it chilled her standing in the cemetery up to Honey Creek Church.

Mama told me the story about how she got that cotton dress she was wearing when she died. She'd been working at the icehouse early, cooking a big kettle of brown beans and getting bread ready for the lunch run. Clara, the Mexican woman who swept the floors and washed the pots and plates, was sitting on the stool beside the back door watching a dog dig through the trash for scraps. Clara called Mama over to look, and together they watched that dog wrestle with something that had spoiled and been tossed. It was wedged under a pallet. The dog was whining and dripping spit because he could smell the meat.

Clara laughed, but Mama didn't watch for long before she did something. She didn't like to see dogs begging or whining for food, not since the time my father made Nicklaus crawl round begging like a dog to get his supper. She walked out to the rubbish heap and shifted things to get the pallet off the meat. She didn't see the pile of garbage start falling. The trash heap fell and some of it spilled against her leg, messing up her dress.

I asked her what she'd been thinking about that she wasn't paying attention to the garbage and she said: "I guess I was thinking about you kids out to the country place. How, around that time, you would be stirring a pot of cornmeal to feed the little ones before they walked up the road to meet the school bus. How Nicklaus would be laying in, trying to sleep until your father would drag him out to carry cedar poles. How you would slip Nicklaus a few pieces of bread and some pork fat as he slipped out the door while Herbert would carry your father's lunch tin full of sausage and beans."

When my mama and Clara had finished laughing (and the dog had run off with that hindquarter), they went back inside the kitchen, and Clara pulled the cotton dress from her bag. It was a new work dress Clara had bought to take to her daughter later in the day. Mama washed it that night, but in the morning Clara wouldn't take it: "It's your trash dress, now," she told Mama. "You wear it whenever you feel like helping *perros bravos* get their breakfast."

Mama wore that thing around the trailer all the time. I guess it reminded her of the years when she had rented that room in town and stayed there all week by herself to work at the icehouse.

When I put the gray dress with the piping back into the closet and slid it aside, I saw the next one was the black thing Aunt Frieda gave her to wear to Tony-boy's christening. She wore that one twice — once to the baptism, and a second time eleven months later for Tony-boy's burial. After that, she hung it in the closet with this other cold dress.

I sat there on her bed and thought about the way new clothes always meant sadness for my mother. After all those funerals, how could new dresses bring her joy? They had become memories woven into the shape of clothes. Time had a way of ticking off the bodies of the people she knew like they were seconds on a clock. To my mother those new dresses were woven out of tears and sadness. After she stopped working, she never liked to wear new clothes, and she never wore them until the men at Doeppenschmidt's had to wash her cold body and dress it for the last time.

Ben's Paintings

To this point, my grandfather has emerged as little more than a harsh patriarch, but I keep coming up against things that don't quite fit with that image. I'm not satisfied to let such a one-sided view stand, not so much out of loyalty to an ancestor, but because such simplification hides more than it reveals about a person or a place. My grandfather was a bitter and hard person much of the time, but he was also a fine musician who played the fiddle simply for the joy of it. He also made many paintings that demonstrate a clear awareness and attention to the world around him. This is something that gets erased when critics categorize and analyze such works as "folk art." There is more in his paintings than simply a fresh or unjaded or primitive view of the world painted by someone with more desire to create than technical skill to paint. In such artwork I see an example of the very real need for attention to the details of the places in which we live.

I've already talked about one of my grandfather's paintings—the one of the little boy tossing his ball into the air—but there are many others around. A few of them hung on the wall of H & B's Texas Style Bar-B-Q, a restaurant in Nebraska once owned by Uncle Benny and Uncle Herbert. Most of the paintings are of animals and plants common to the Hill Country. I mention this because I think it speaks something of Opa Ben's connection to the environment in which he lived. He spent much of his working life outdoors—stretching fence, clearing brush, making charcoal—and would have had lots of time to observe the animals and landscapes around him.

He would cut animals out of wood using a form he had drawn, and then sit for hours carefully painting with a brush each feather of a road-runner's wing. He painted armadillos, and each segment of the arma-dillo's nine-banded back would be clearly delineated, the overlapping bands fitting together like brickwork to make up the animal's protective shell. His cactus have hundreds of individual spines, just like the ones I see growing among the pitted limestones when I go up to the shack.

"He usually painted on wood, right?" I asked during one visit.

"No, that was toward the end, and he wasn't doing that for artwork, he was doing that for something else. But he would paint all that by hand on those [carved wood] roadrunners, those armadillos, those are all painted by hand. The crosses. He was going to go into business with that, but the oils, they took him a long time."

"They are oils, aren't they? They're not acrylics?"

"Right. They were done with oils. Yeah. All those paintings are oils. I don't know what paints he used on the animals. He would sit there with his brush and put all the shells of the armadillo on. So each one *was* a personal painting."

"You want to know what kind of paints they are," Aunt Barbara said. "You go over there and look in that refrigerator that's by that shed that we built over Mama's trailer, that's where his paints are."

"I've never seen any of the animals, like the armadillos. They were wood carvings?"

"Yeah. They were cut out of wood, and then he would paint, color the armadillos. That's a wonder we don't have one, Mama?"

"Yeah, there's one over on top of the TV," Aunt Barbara pointed out.

"There, is that one?" I pointed at a small carved armadillo set into a wooden base. "Is that the kind of thing you're talking about?"

"No. They hang with chains. They were four times that big," Uncle Herbert said. "That's one of his." He pointed to the wooden armadillo on the television. "That's one that's not even painted yet. He didn't fin-ish that one. They were hung on two little chains. They would hang from the ceiling and they would turn around and around. He had roadrunners and he had all kinds of little characters. There's one of his birds there on the wall. It's got a broken off leg, but that was a flying bird right there. See how it has all the painting on it. He never really got big in the busi-ness. He died before he could. He was always going to make 'big money' at it. Dreamer."

"He had a lot of different schemes for making money?"

"Yeah. He did, but he had a lot of talent. But he wasted it, because —I think that was partially because of us. To give us the basic survival needs."

"He had to do other things?"

"He had to go work for a living instead of exercising his qualities as a painter or musician."

Incest

I've waited until now to retell my Aunt Barbara's telling of the following story because I want this emotional tale to fit in where it belongs— woven into the middle of the common cloth of any other daily story or activity. The topic of incest is highly charged in the United States. In families where it has occurred, psychologists often act as if incest explains all the problems. Aunt Angie once said to me in frustration: "It seems like that number is always coming up, as if it answered all the problems." "What number?" I asked. "What do you mean?" "That incest number. Everybody seems to think incest caused all their problems."

Aunt Angie's words point out that painful memories are only part of the story. For many years I have been unable to heal the angry memories and broken emotions that have arisen from the poison of my father's incestuous abuse of my older sister. My preoccupation with that traumatic event blocked my growth as a man. While I still lived "at home" with my parents and sisters, I guess I tried to be someone who could soar above it all and be safe. Then, at fifteen I broke away from my parents and sisters and chose, with the help of my mother's mother and my mother's sister, to spend the next six or seven years isolated from these people, this closed nuclear family environment of the American Dream that contains such explosive emotional forces.

When I renewed my contact with the Syrings, my father's side of the family, I discovered aunts and uncles who taught me the value of storytelling and memory as a path to healing. Aunt Barbara and Uncle Herbert talk about the harrowing experiences of rape and incest that have plagued the women of my family for generations, but they tell these traumatic stories in the midst of all the others, in the everydayness of their lives. The juxtaposition of humor, pain, frustration, desire, and good will in their lives and stories has shown me how healing might take place.

The way the stories flow, one into another, sometimes incongruously, points to the way that telling stories (bringing past events into an intelligible relationship with the present) affects our current selves, but does not necessarily limit or simplistically determine them. Barbara's way of being, her way of speaking, acknowledges the past and its power without letting it rule or crush her. She has been ill, yet she is a healer. She speaks about incest, but only as part of a cultural world shaped by poverty in which people remain human, at least so long as all kinds of stories are remembered. Opa Ben was a hard man who abused his children, but he was also a creative man who painted and played music well. He was a man in an impossible financial situation with fourteen children and no access to wealth, or to contraception given his Catholic upbringing—a man who died stricken in a cancer bed, wasted away to half his usual body weight.

The following conversation includes three people: Aunt Barbara, her daughter, Dawn, and myself. We were talking around the kitchen table at Aunt Barbara's on the weekend following a cousin's wedding.

"There are some other, seedier details and stories," Aunt Barbara said.

"Everybody else knows about them, Mom," Dawn said.

"Why not, huhm?"

"*I* know about it," Dawn said.

"You know about it?" Aunt Barbara asked.

"I know about it."

"When did you find out?"

"Aunt Annie told me."

"Oh? She unburdened . . ."

"I think I've actually heard some of this story," I said to set her at ease.

"He molested . . . Virginia," Aunt Barbara said.

"He molested Aunt Annie," Dawn said.

"Yeah, Angie too," Aunt Barbara agreed. "I wouldn't be surprised if he molested all of them."

"I think he molested Aunt Marty," Dawn added. "Just her attitude says it."

"But she doesn't talk about it?" I asked.

"She's not . . . she's just . . . ," Dawn faltered.

"I don't think she remembers it," Aunt Barbara said. "I honestly don't think she remembers it. I think that's a major part of her problem. Her problem . . . she's really got a block on it."

"When this sort of activity that Opa Ben was perpetrating on his daughters . . . was it talked about?" I asked. "Did grandma know? Did she know but not admit it to herself?"

"I think she found out because Virginia thought she was pregnant," Aunt Barbara said.

"Oh, God!"

"That's how she found out. And things never did settle back between them afterwards."

"Between Oma and Opa?"

"She could . . . it was always a problem, yeah. Opa . . . Oma had gone when she was a young girl. She was in a convent for a while."

"I didn't know that," I said. "In San Antonio?"

"Yeah. After she left the convent she went to work for a couple in San Antonio, and from what I understand she was molested there."

"By the man from the couple?" I asked.

"Yeah. Something to that effect. I'm not sure of the details. And Opa never let her live that down. He threw that in her face all the time."

"You mean he acted as if it was her fault?" I asked.

"Yeah. I mean she was a young girl . . ."

"That's such a typical attitude in this culture, that rape is a woman's own fault," I said.

"Yeah, he never let her live it down."

"I guess she didn't have a lot of choice, though," I said. "What could she do after she found out about him doing this to her daughters? If they were having a rough time making a living . . ."

"Well, she was working in New Braunfels and they were still living in Kendalia. And she would go back home on the weekends, you know. I said I thought that Virginia thought she was pregnant—that's not how it came out, either, come to think of it. She surprised him at home."

"And she caught him?"

"She came home and caught him. *That's* how she found out now that I remember. It took a long time before I found out how she found out. And when she told me, she said, 'I came in when I wasn't supposed to. I came home on a weekday. I got the chance to come home, and I caught them.'"

"What'd she do?" Dawn asked. "Nothing, I'll bet."

"Well, if I remember right, what she told me she did is she got a garden hose and she let Opa have it with the garden hose. So I don't think he ever hit her, but she hit him," Barbara said and laughed.

"She should have hit him harder!" I said and we all laughed.

"She . . . I think she let him have it with everything she had in her. And like I said, it was really a strained time from then on."

Abuse

Aunt Barbara and Uncle Herbert tell painful stories at times. Much hurt and anger in my family stems from the figure of Opa Ben, who abused his children. Uncle Herbert, however, tells the story in such a way that it opens up the past and seeks to understand how problems sometimes result as much from cultural constructions as from the vagaries of personal temperament. Opa Ben beat his children, and it is likely that he did so for reasons unique to his personality, but he also lived in a cultural environment where men were made to assume the role of discipline-maker and punishment-giver. Given this constructed social reality, Opa Ben's heavy hand had some official sanction.

His obligation to punish put him into the role of the "bad guy," perhaps creating a situation where an inner poison was made manifest in the social world. As Uncle Herbert tells the story, my grandmother, deferring to the cultural role of the patriarch of the family, would wait until Opa Ben had returned at the end of the day. Then the children would be lined up and presented for punishment by his hand. "By the end of the day," Uncle Herbert observes, "80 percent of everybody had a whipping lined up . . . so you can imagine what that made him feel like. He was obligated to do his 'duty' and beat all of us, whether he wanted to or not."

With an awareness of the cultural pressures that affected Opa Ben, Uncle Herbert has moved into a consciousness of his own role as a father. He has learned from his father's mistakes, and worked to avoid repeating them in the raising of his own children.

"Angeline got abused tremendously because of her weight problem. *Feta sow* is how . . . ," Uncle Herbert said one morning while we talked.

"*Feta sow?*" I asked.

"*Feta sow,* 'fat pig,'" Uncle Herbert explained. "Or 'female pig.' *Feta sow* is what he would call her. And look at my father [Opa Ben was a large man who once weighed more than three hundred pounds]. Your father, because he was always getting into trouble, my daddy embarrassed him to no end. He would make him come in from the living area outside and crawl all the way to the table before he was allowed to eat. And one time, he fed him under the table, as a dog. That was punishment, along with a whipping. Like if I punish my son, I would ground him and things like that. But he made your father crawl like that from outside."

"That's not punishment. That's just sheer humiliation."

"So now you can probably see why your own father has problems too," Uncle Herbert concluded.

"Well, I've heard that story from my dad, but I wasn't sure if that was an exaggeration."

"No. When I sat at that table, he would have us all sitting around that table and then he would force your dad to crawl all the way in when he did things wrong. And your father was notorious at getting into trouble. But the more he got in, the worse it got. And at age ten or twelve he run off from home, run off into the pasture, left home. And Daddy'd be hollering on after him, 'LAUS! NICK-LAUS!' He'd be hollering for him, and your dad would be hiding right down the hill and wouldn't come back home. About three in the morning he would sneak back and lay in one of the old junk cars we had. Mother would find him, and then she would get him, somehow, back into the house, and Daddy would, on occasion, let it go. But if he got ahold of you at the time, he'd whip your ass. And Mother was probably just as at fault. She'd say, 'You just wait till your daddy gets home.' I told Barbara, 'Don't you ever tell my kids that. If they need punishment, you take care of it right then. I don't want to be the bad boy.'"

"And now he fusses at me because I do that," Aunt Barbara says and laughs.

"Yeah, you're supposed to punish them. But I didn't mean throw them out of the house!" Uncle Herbert says and laughs.

This is a reference to an event that took place earlier in the day. Aunt Barbara told her son, Kevin, that he had to move from his room in the mobile home to a camper parked beside the butchering shed. She was weary of tending the needs of her twenty-year-old, nearly adult child. Kevin had been promising to join the military—a common move in my family as an attempt to get steady employment—but he had been reluctant to take the final step of enlisting. Aunt Barbara hoped that the move to the camper might provide Kevin with the impetus to go through with his plans. Throughout the day she kept saying, "Mama bird is pushing baby bird out the nest, so he can learn how to fly."

"I meant punishment," Uncle Herbert continues. "I said don't come and say 'You wait till your daddy gets home.' If I set some prerequisite and they've done wrong, then I'll take care of it. But don't, don't do that to them or me. Because first of all, Mother could never catch us to whip us—we'd run away . . . most times you'd run off and you wouldn't come home, and she'd say, 'Wait till Daddy gets home.' So when he got home . . . you eventually had to come home too . . . and he'd line everybody up that needed a whipping that night, and he'd sit there and whip them. By the end of the day, 80 percent of everybody had a whipping lined up, so you can imagine what that made him feel like. He was obligated to do his 'duty.' His saying was '*gehohen mein ocht-und-vierzig.*'"

"*Gehohen . . . ?*" I ask.

"*Gehohen mein ocht-und-vierzig,*" Uncle Herbert says. "'Go get my forty-eight-incher.' And the forty-eight-incher was his belt. And it hung on the nail right next to the kitchen door. And draped, it looked like three miles long, you know. [laughs] And when he was going to get that, means you was going to get a strapping, and when he whipped you, there wasn't . . . he didn't aim for the cheeks. It was the lower back—"

"Owww! There's no padding there!"

"Yeah. Welts that long . . . no padding, the welts, and it hurt more. The lower back's more sensitive than the butt. And we would go to school . . . course, he would get it anywhere, because the tendency was to try to block him after a while, because you'd climb under the table, and he was beating you under the table too. But you would go to school with big . . . your dad many a time went with welts. The end of the belt would leave a V shape like that. [spreads his fingers into a gesture] Bloody most here [indicates the point of the V], and then mellow out further up. We'd go to school with all those stripes. Because you got a lot of whipping. So I got them too, but your dad got more of them. Because he got more trouble. Daddy would say to him, 'Being the oldest, you know better, so you get it.'"

"Aunt Barbara was telling me last night, that at some point Opa Ben would get tired of whipping, so he'd have the kids whip each other."

"Angeline," Uncle Herbert affirms. "Angeline was the one who had to do the beating. She hated to whip us. Nicklaus did some whipping too, but it was mostly Angeline had to do the whipping, because . . . and Daddy would stand there and watch her do it."

"And if she didn't do it hard enough?" I ask.

"He'd whip her. And that was not because he was tired. He just got, sexually or otherwise, gratified from seeing her whip us. And we had to come back there and take a lick, and it would be 'WHOP! Dittyditty-dittydo.' [He gestures as if he were a child running away with hands covering his butt.] You'd run over there, and he'd say, 'Come on over here. If you don't come back, you get two more licks.' You got to get back there, and 'WHAP!' she'd give another one. But she never did like it, because it made her feel guilty, and if she didn't do it hard enough, then she'd get a whipping for not doing it hard enough. And, yeah, he was tired of dishing out punishment, and that's true, but there were times when he wasn't tired of it, he just . . . wanted someone else to be doing the whipping. And Angeline, who was the oldest girl and responsible for raising the younger ones, Angeline had to do it then."

Other Voices

For me—a writer in the last quarter of the twentieth century, not much more than a hundred years after Emancipation, a writer who is black and a woman—the exercise is very different. My job becomes how to rip that veil drawn over "proceedings too terrible to relate."

Moving that veil aside requires, therefore, certain things. First of all, I must trust my own recollections. I must also depend on the recollections of others. Thus memory weighs heavily in what I write, in how I begin and in what I find significant. Zora Neale Hurston said, "Like dead-seeming cold rocks, I have memories within that came out of the material that went to make me." These "memories within" are the subsoil of my work. But memories and recollections won't give me total access to the unwritten interior life of these people. Only the act of the imagination can help me.

Toni Morrison, "The Site of Memory"

Annie's Ghosts

Tony-boy was hungry tonight.

Some nights he left Annie alone and she slept straight through until dawn. But tonight he was there, hungry and sucking and wanting more and more. Annie sat up from the bed and pulled her housecoat on. Tony-boy hungry meant Annie sleepless.

David didn't hear her wake up. He never slept long—the doctor wanted to put a tracheal tube in his neck, but David refused, so he was always waking himself up gasping for breath. Someday he would smother himself, that extra bit of flesh in his throat would cut off his air and David wouldn't get up again. He rarely slept for more than a few hours at a time, but when he slept, he was gone, deeper than Annie ever saw anyone else sleep. He slept the way Annie remembered her babies sleeping.

Tony-boy sucked and sucked until her ribs hurt. She rose from the bed and went into the kitchen and still Tony-boy sucked.

"Tonight's a hard one, is it, Tony-boy?"

The sucking grew stronger, pulling more. Annie fell into a chair and lay her head on the table, struggling for breath.

"I know, I know." She could barely speak. "Cold there, ain't it? I'm giving most of what I got left. You want to suck me empty?"

The insistent tug let up a little, enough for Annie to pull shallow quick breaths. She got up to make a pot of tea. The white dog lay in the grass out back. He was awake, she knew, and watching her through the sliding glass door. His eyes were hidden in the dark beneath his brow, but the rest of his white body glowed in the moonlight.

"Dog-ghost, you going to just sit there and let me suffocate?"

She carried her cup out onto the patio and dropped down into a chair. The dog perked up its ears, but didn't move from its spot. Annie sipped her tea with eyes closed and waited for the sucking to stop. Near dawn it finally ceased. The white dog had fallen asleep.

She remembered how it had been at first when Tony-boy'd been satisfied with her milk. After each of her boys was born, Tony-boy would come in the night to get her milk. She had started breastfeeding her oldest, but Tony-boy's visits ended that. Her milk turned bitter, at least Chris acted that way, and he would spit out her nipple and cry. She tried for two days to get him to take it in his mouth, growing more frantic each time he cried and spit. After he refused to eat on the third morning, Annie asked Oma Relia for an old bottle. None of her boys ever drank her milk after that.

So Tony-boy had it all. Four times Annie had had milk, and four times he came to take it. Even after her little girl had come stillborn,

Annie's breasts swelled up, and Tony-boy visited every night. Annie even wanted and needed his visits then, during the aftermath of Kimberley's stillbirth.

But then Tony-boy had grown more bold. Annie hadn't had milk for ten years, and Tony-boy got hungrier and hungrier. So he started sucking her breath. He started gently at first, barely taking more than what she breathed out anyhow. In some ways, she preferred this, it was easier to just breathe. She could smell him close by her face, under her nose, at her lips, taking what she exhaled, plus a little extra.

A little extra at first. Then he started taking a little extra more. One night she awoke with a weight on her chest, pressing down as if the cat had jumped up there. But when she shook herself awake she knew it was him, all soft-smelling and milk-breathed. He drank her breath in small gulps, a thirsty cat lapping water, and she started struggling for air. The white dog lay at the foot of the bed that night, and he started growling, still asleep but twitching. That night it had been enough, and Tony-boy went away, frightened by the dog-ghost. She remembered that one of her aunts had told her that sometimes a loved one's spirit would return in the form of a white dog to protect you, so for several years thereafter, Annie made sure the white dog lay on the foot of her bed before she fell asleep. That way, the dog-ghost would chase Tony-boy off before it got too bad.

Annie sat in the chair on the patio and watched the sunrise and remembered. She remembered the way she had first given Tony-boy her breath. Her father had taken the other children to tend the charcoal kilns, and Annie was to cook and mind little Tony-boy. Oma Relia had already gone back to working in town, so Annie was alone at the country place.

Tony-boy was a good baby, crying only when he needed changing, and smiling already when he was only a few months old. Remembering back, Annie thought she probably loved him best of all her younger siblings, but she wasn't sure whether she remembered that way because Tony-boy had never grown up; she'd never had to beat Tony-boy while Opa Ben stood by watching to see that Annie was swinging hard enough.

The morning had been cold, so Annie pulled the quilts off her father's bed and covered Tony-boy with a warm nest while she went out to get wood for the stove. She had the beans bubbling in the pot and cornbread in the oven before she thought it might be time for Tony-boy to be awake and wanting to eat. She knew he would never cry to be fed, only when he was wet. She went into the back room and pulled the quilts away from her brother's tiny body.

Tony-boy was blue. His tiny fingers clenched the edge of a quilt, but his arms hadn't been strong enough to push the smothering covers away. His face had the color of bluebonnets in bloom.

Annie had no idea how long Tony-boy had been still, but she never doubted she could put breath back into his body. She lifted him from the blankets and carried him to the kitchen where it was warmer. Lying on the table he looked like porcelain. Lowering her mouth to his face, Annie smelled the milk in his mouth and nostrils. She started to breath, slowly and steadily while she rubbed Tony-boy's tiny toes with her fingers.

Annie stayed bent over that table for an hour, giving her breath to her brother even after his lungs had begun rising and falling again on their own. In the evening, Opa Ben slapped her for burning the bread and wasting flour, but that was one blow Annie knew she deserved, though her father would never know why. When Tony-boy's breath stopped in his sleep a few nights later, Annie knew she had been wrong not to give Tony-boy everything, every last breath she had left in her body.

The white dog wouldn't come inside the house at night no more. David thought it was because he had stepped on the dog's paw too many times when he got up from the table, but Annie knew that white dog wasn't afraid of anything her husband could do to it. That dog-ghost was feeling too old to be messing with Tony-boy anymore. That was the bad thing about dog-ghosts—they got old just like a person. Tony-boy never got older, never would. That dog-ghost would curl up and die one day, and Tony-boy would still be coming, trying to take back all those breaths that his sister Annie had stolen; and Annie, certain that she'd unintentionally taken them, waited nearly every night to give them back, bit by bit, to her little brother.

Two Moments of Commentary on Storytelling

1. Toni Morrison

Fiction, by definition, is distinct from fact. Presumably it's the product of imagination—invention—and it claims the freedom to dispense with "what really happened," or where it really happened, or when it really happened, and nothing needs to be publicly verifiable, although much of it can be verified. . . .

The work I do frequently falls, in the minds of most people, into the realm of fiction called fantastic, or mythic, or magical, or unbelievable. I'm not comfortable with these labels. I consider that my single gravest responsibility (in spite of that magic) is not to lie. When I hear someone say, "Truth is stranger than fiction," I think that old chestnut is truer than we know, because it doesn't say that truth is truer than fiction; just that it's stranger, meaning that it's odd. It may be excessive, it may be more interesting, but the important thing is that it's random—and fiction is not random.

Therefore, the crucial distinction for me is not the difference between fact and fiction, but the distinction between fact and truth. Because facts can exist without human intelligence, but truth cannot.

"The Site of Memory"

2. Uncle Herbert

"You may, at some point, rewrite the stories," Uncle Herbert says one evening while we're drinking coffee and talking.

"Yeah, I do that," I tell him. "That's what I'm doing with these short stories, retelling the family stories with my imagination inserted. And what I think I'm doing with that is trying to bring out some of the 'facts' that don't get contained, that don't get brought forward by simply transcribing the story, by taking the oral form and just putting it on paper. There are certain things that I know because of my knowledge of the family, and because of my knowledge of the family situation, that don't get brought forward if I don't construct an imaginative framework for it. So that's what I think I'm doing in the writing."

"You see what I'm saying," Uncle Herbert says. "You're studying the facts and trying to get more facts into the story. Not just the story. To bring more into the story to make it more realistic, and more factual about the story."

"But what do you think facts are?" I ask. "Some of my stories are not 'factual.' I've written this one story that's basically about Aunt Angie and her feelings about Tony-boy. She feels a lot of guilt, I think, both because she was told that she killed him in some way, and because she had the responsibility for caring for him and the rest of you. I think she might feel like she failed in some way. So I'm writing this story trying to get at how she carries this burden, even to this day. But I can't just say that, it's too . . . it doesn't evoke the feeling, it doesn't do what a story does . . . "

"Inspire the reader to think," he says.

"So what I've done is," I continue, "I have Aunt Angie being haunted by Tony-boy's ghost. And he comes back when she's much older, he keeps coming back, and he steals her breath. He starts out stealing her milk when she has babies, but then he steals her breath."

"But then are you calling it a 'novel'? or are you calling it . . . what are you calling it?"

"Well, right now it's part of a novel, but I think that it's trying to get at the subjective experience that Aunt Angie has. I think she feels that way. Whether or not it's actually a ghost or not. It could just be memories; memories are ghosts of another sort."

"But are you calling this a novel based on facts, or is it just a novel of writings?" he asks.

"It's . . . it's . . . I don't know what exactly it is. 'Ethnography' tries to tell the story of what is there. I consider this fiction that I'm writing a part of my ethnography. I consider it a part of what is really there. That, in my opinion, is what Aunt Angie feels about Tony-boy."

"We all have that . . . me, in all actuality, at Tony-boy's death, I lied," he says.

"You lied? How so?"

"Because everybody wanted attention at that particular time. And they were trying to determine when he actually died. And I had told a story. I slept on the floor, not on the bed with everybody, all eight others who slept up there. I said that he had got off the bed during the night, and I said he fell off the bed during the night and that I put him back on the bed, which I didn't. Why I said this story, I don't know, but it was a lie."

"He didn't get off the bed? You were just trying to get attention for yourself?"

"I don't know why I did it," he says. "But I did. Because everybody was looking for something to say about when they had seen him last. And I said that, and it was never truth."

"Did you ever tell anybody that you lied?"

Nickolaus Syring (far right) with brass band, circa 1910–1920. Nickolaus was the author's great-grandfather.

The Children of Heinrich Syring on the day of Nickolaus Syring's funeral, April 2, 1923. Nickolaus, their brother, died of stomach cancer when he was 47. From left: Anna, Ferdinand, Thekla, Theodore, Ida, Margaretha, Emelie, Mary, Joseph, Henry, Jr.

Eva Syring (nee Kunz), the author's great-grandmother, circa 1927. Her husband's early death left her alone to raise their ten surviving children and to manage the family's ranch of nearly nine hundred acres.

The Alex Scheel Family, circa 1920. From left: Ewald, Bonifacious, Alex, Laura (nee Hildebrandt) holding Clara, Otilia, Aurelia (the author's grandmother, Oma Aurelia, in text).

The Eva Syring family, 1931. Standing in back row (from left): Lucia, Nancy Cooley, Frieda, Hulda, Alfred, Ella, Valentine, Fritz Hoffmann, Benjamin (author's grandfather, Opa Ben, in text), Paul; Seated: Helen, Eva, Bertha (holding Helen Hoffmann); Children in front: Edna Kruse, Edward Kruse, Herman Hoffmann.

Some of Eva's children with the truck called "The Puhteetah," circa 1920. Standing in back: Helen, Alfred; In front: Ben, Lucia, Paul.

Ben and Lucia on running board. Behind is the repair/blacksmith shop on the Syring place, circa 1920.

Some of Eva's children in winter, circa 1920. From left: Helen, Ben, Paul, Lucia, Ella.

Some of Eva's children in front of the ranch house, circa 1923. Probably taken around the time their father, Nickolaus, died. From left: Paul, Hulda, Frieda, Ella, Helen, Ben, Bertha.

Lucia and the garden in front of the ranch house, circa 1925.

Ella with chickens at the side of the house, circa 1923.

Ben (author's grandfather) with accordion and dog, 1927.

Ben and Lucia, 1929.

Ella and Ben, circa 1931.

Paul, Lucia, Ben, circa 1931.

Ben and Paul with hunting dogs and raccoon, possum, ringtail, and fox pelts, circa 1932.

Ben, circa 1942, probably taken a year or two after he and Aurelia
were married.

Eva Syring (at center of back row) with some of her grandchildren, 1948. Author's father is the boy in the white shirt, second from right in middle row. Author's Aunt Angie and Uncle Herbert are on far right of front row.

Ben (at center with fiddle) leading the band performing at Angeline's (Annie in text) twenty-first birthday party, 1961. Author's father, Nickolaus, is at right with guitar.

"No."

"This is the first time that you ever said anything?"

"Yeah. I never said anything. Nobody ever contested it, because I think they were at the time trying to come up with their own story about when they'd last remembered him. And I never said anything about it, and I remembered it when you was talking about Angie and Tony-boy."

"My question, then, is," I say, returning to our earlier line of talk. "Is there a truth in what I've written about Aunt Angie feeling haunted? Maybe all you who were kids feel haunted by that memory, the memory of his death?"

"Probably some basical truth."

"So what is it? Is it not a 'fact'?" I ask.

"No. But it's like the writer there," he says about a Barry Lopez essay, "Landscape and Narrative," from which I'd just read a passage to him. "He's writing about the *way* these guys tell stories, not so much what they're saying. But in your story, you're trying to write the way she thinks, that's a little different. So you got to base your knowledge on factual information to start with. He's actually writing a novel, or a book . . ."

"It's a short essay," I offer.

"He's writing *about* the storyteller. And you're trying to put your mind in her mind, and write her feelings intelligibly, so people can understand them. Where you think she was standing at. She can't tell you whether that's the way . . . that's why it's a story. But it's, again, your interpretation of the story. It's not hers, because she hasn't said it."

Notes on an Easter Sunday

Late in the afternoon, long after the hamburgers, chicken breasts, and hot dogs have been grilled and the sweet rice and beans eaten, Aunt Barbara arrives with her daughter, Dawn, and one of Dawn's friends. They had not planned to join the Syring family for the holiday because Aunt Barbara's mother and sisters were having a picnic of their own, but the other party had been unsuccessful and broken up early. I'm happy to see her because I wanted to talk to her about the writings I've been doing based on our conversations, and also to thank her for everything she has already taught me about herself, my family, and myself.

Aunt Barbara's arm is stiff—she can't even raise it parallel to the floor. This is the same pain she had at the healing service at Our Lady of Lourdes in San Antonio. The healer prayed for her that night, and she said the pain had been eased, but the stiffness remained. Now the pain and the stiffness have both returned.

A short while after Aunt Barbara's arrival, Aunt Virginia—who considers herself a healer and is part of a healing team at another church in San Antonio—comes into the garage where I am sitting with Uncle Robert and Uncle Stephen. The three of us have been trying to remember how to play *shafkopf,* an old German card game that my grandparents and great-grandparents played. When I was young I often sat beside my father, Great-uncle Godfried, and Gross-opa Scheel while they played this game on the patio behind Gross-opa's house in San Antonio. Uncle Stephen said he remembered how to play, but when we sat down with the deck of cards, his memory proved a bit incomplete, and we are trying, between the three of us, to remember the rules. Aunt Virginia, who says she remembers exactly how to play, offers her explanation of the rules and the hierarchy of the cards, then she asks Uncle Stephen if he will help her and Aunt Angie pray for Aunt Barbara. We finish the hand we are trying to play, then move out onto the back patio.

In the back yard, a few of the older children are hiding Easter eggs, the plastic kind filled with candy because Aunt Schatze says: "They'll just break the hardboiled ones, anyway, and then they won't eat them." The hiders are not being too crafty, and bright plastic eggs are scattered over the muddy grass.

"Maybe we should wait to pray until after the egg hunt," Aunt Angie says.

But Aunt Virginia tells Aunt Barbara to stand off to one side of the patio. Uncle Stephen pushes the sliding glass door closed to reduce the noise coming from the poker game going on at the kitchen table inside. I am sitting off to one side with about ten other relatives. I'm all prepared to be the dutiful anthropologist, to watch the healing ceremony from a distance and take mental notes, when Aunt Barbara looks over and says, "David, will you help pray with me?"

Aunt Virginia positions herself in front of Aunt Barbara. Uncle Stephen stands to one side, while Aunt Angie, tired because she only slept for an hour last night after sitting up with Aunt Schatze to decorate cakes, sits in a chair next to Aunt Barbara. I stand behind Aunt Barbara and rest my hands on her shoulders.

Aunt Virginia opens a small vial of holy oil and anoints Aunt Angie's wrists and forehead while asking God to grant Aunt Angie the privilege to serve as his vessel of healing. She moves on to Uncle Stephen, then to me, and finally to Aunt Barbara.

Aunt Virginia tells Aunt Barbara to raise her arms in front of her, a posture which the healer at Our Lady of Lourdes also used with each person seeking healing. Aunt Barbara's right arm doesn't come up as far as her left.

"What's the matter with your arm, Barbara!" Aunt Virginia says, and to me her tone sounds more like a rebuke than a question.

"That's what hurts," says Aunt Barbara. "I can't raise it any higher. I haven't been able to for a while. I even had to have Dawn wash my hair for me this morning." She has tears in her eyes.

Aunt Virginia tells her to lower her arm, and begins to pray, first some general invocations to God to let Aunt Barbara receive his healing touch, then she moves on and says the Our Father.

Uncle Stephen prays as well, often repeating, "Thank you, Jesus," "in Jesus' name," amidst his supplication. Aunt Angie, sitting in her chair, rests her hands on Aunt Barbara's knees and prays inaudibly to herself. I stand behind Aunt Barbara, rest my palms on her shoulders, and take slow deep breaths, the kind of breathing I've learned from yoga instruction during the last few months.

Aunt Virginia repeats the Our Father a few times, and begins to work on the healing. She touches Aunt Barbara's arm and asks where it hurts. "Here," Aunt Barbara says and gestures to her right shoulder and upper chest. Aunt Virginia lays her hand on the place and says more "Our Fathers," closes her eyes, and begins speaking in her Prayer Tongue. It sounds similar to the Tongue of the male healer I saw at Our Lady of Lourdes. Aunt Virginia hesitates a moment, makes a decision, and says: "Spirit of Evil, Spirit of Pain, I take authority over you. I order you to leave Barbara's left shoulder—" She stops a moment in confusion. "It is her left shoulder, isn't it?" From where I stand behind Aunt Barbara, my body is aligned the same way, so I say, "It's her right shoulder." Aunt Virginia continues, "I order you to leave Barbara's right shoulder." She speaks again in her Prayer Tongue.

After a moment, she stops and says, "Raise your arms, Barbara."

Aunt Barbara raises her arms, and again the right one does not come up as high as the left.

"What's binding you, Barbara?" says Aunt Virginia. "There's something bothering you, what is it?"

"I'm nervous about school," says Aunt Barbara. She has been taking classes at a community college. When she arrived at the party, I asked how classes were going, and Aunt Barbara had said, "I got my first book report back and got an A-plus, I liked to have fell out of my chair." I asked, "What book was it about?" "Mother Angelica's book about miracles."

Aunt Virginia is not satisfied with Aunt Barbara's response. "There must be something else. What else is bothering you?"

Aunt Barbara pauses a moment, then says, "I went to the doctor last week about my shoulder. He gave me a steroid shot. I'm supposed to go see him again Friday. If it doesn't get better they're going to give me another mammogram."

Still Aunt Virginia seems dissatisfied. "Isn't there something else? Something else you're worried about? You don't have to say it, just think about it."

But Aunt Barbara persists: "I'm afraid the silicon has leaked. Maybe that's why my arm hurts."

Aunt Virginia refuses to accept this answer, and she begins praying again. "Pray with me, Barbara," she urges:

Dear Father, forgive me, Barbara, for my anger at those who have hurt me . . .

Aunt Barbara remains quiet. "Repeat after me," Aunt Virginia commands:

Dear Father, forgive me, Barbara, for my anger at those who have hurt me . . . "

Dear Father, forgive me, Barbara, for my anger at those who have hurt me . . .

And forgive those who have hurt me . . .
And forgive those who have hurt me . . .

Give me strength not to hate those who have hurt me . . .
Give me strength not to hate those who have hurt me . . .

As Aunt Barbara echoes Aunt Virginia, I think of an article I'd read the previous morning. A woman in a neighboring state became frustrated with her insurance company. She had developed lupus and lymphatic cancer as the result of silicon leaks from breast implants, but the insurance company had refused to pay for their removal. They called the surgery "cosmetic." The woman, wanting the silicon out of her body, had used a razor blade to open an incision, and squeezed her breast to remove as much silicon as possible before she passed out. When she awoke, she repeated the procedure on the other breast. I wondered whether Aunt Barbara had heard about this on television.

Aunt Virginia says: "Something's not right. Somebody here doesn't believe. Is there anybody here who doesn't believe this is happening? Is there anybody here who doesn't believe we can do this healing?"

She looks over to the table where a few relatives are sitting. Most of them are Opa Ben and Oma Aurelia's grandchildren between the ages of ten and seventeen. No one responds.

"This is important," says Aunt Virginia severely. "Is there anybody here who doesn't believe?"

Uncle Robert, who has been sitting by the table, says to the grandchildren, "It's all right if you don't. It's no reflection on you. All you have to do is get up and go inside."

Aunt Virginia looks directly at one of her own children, "Do you believe?" The child, annoyed, says a short "Yes."

I wonder about my own position, standing behind Aunt Barbara. I'm part of the healing group closest to her body. Am I the one who's obstructing the ceremony? I take deep breaths and try to think of nothing but the sound of the air in my nostrils.

Aunt Virginia begins praying again—supplications to God, her Prayer Tongue, and more Our Fathers. After a few minutes, she pauses. I think of my conversations with Aunt Barbara about the alleged appearance of Mary at Medjugorie, about Aunt Barbara's special reverence for Mary. "Ask for Mary's intercession," I say. Aunt Virginia ignores me and says another Our Father.

Aunt Angie gets up from her chair and goes into the house. The young children, who have been ordered to wait inside until the prayer is finished, crowd by the sliding door, their faces pressed against the glass as they look out at the eggs scattered in the grass.

Aunt Virginia says, "Say the prayer, David."

I recite:

Hail Mary full of grace the Lord is with you. Blessed are you among
women, and blessed is the fruit of thy womb, Jesus. Holy Mary,
Mother of God, pray for us sinners now and at the hour of our
death, amen.

I pause for a moment, but before I can repeat the prayer as is cus-
tomary at this point, Aunt Virginia interrupts with a Gloria Patri, what
my family calls the "Glory Be":

Glory be to the Father, and to the Son, and to the Holy Ghost. As
it was in the beginning, is now, and ever shall be, world without
end, amen.

Aunt Virginia moves me around to the front of Aunt Barbara, ma-
nipulates my body, controls me, and says: "Put your hand on her shoulder, David." I rest my palm lightly on the tense muscle. Aunt Virginia
and Uncle Stephen each rest a hand on my shoulders. Aunt Virginia
continues praying. I keep breathing slow and deep, and again try to con-
centrate on nothing but my breath.

Aunt Angie returns and suggests that we take a break, let Aunt Barbara rest, and let the children go on with their egg hunt. Later that night,
at her own house, Aunt Angie will say to me, "I just wanted to let the
children have their fun. There wasn't any way a healing was going to be
done with all of the anxious, frustrated feelings coming from those children inside." Uncle Robert adds, "You just can't tell little kids to sit still
like that. Besides, that's what Easter's supposed to be for—for the kids."

Machines of Memory

While the modern map is a marvel of efficient geographical commu-
nication, though, in other important ways it does not tell us very
much at all.

Kent C. Ryden, *Mapping the Invisible Landscape*

Antiquing in the Hill Country also lends itself to another fascinating
trail, that being the history of the Hills. Some stores might have
pieces that belonged to the son of the town's founding father, while
another store might have a pie safe that was shipped from Germany,

while another store might have a Biedermeier bedstead made of black walnut. The point is that not only does antiquing in the Hill Country have much to offer in the way of furnishing your home, it also is a means of merging a part of the Hill Country's rich and versatile history into your family's history.

Judith Glasscock, "On the Antiques Trail"

When I started to discover what the shack and the surrounding Hill Country means to me in memory and in current experience, I went out and bought a set of Geological Survey maps for the area including and surrounding the shack. The scale of those surveys is small enough that when I look at the map on my wall, I see an unfilled square representing the shack, and a dotted blue line representing Curry Creek. There are many different kinds of squares on this map.

Solid black squares represent buildings, and purple ones represent buildings added after the original survey date of 1964. In 1982 a resurvey was conducted on the Kendalia Quadrangle (the official quadrangle within which the shack's square rests) using airborne photography, and it was this survey that provided the data for the revised purple squares and lines. I assume the emptiness of the shack's square means that it was determined to be a building that is no longer functional. I don't mind that assessment by the government surveyors. It is better when they assess your buildings as defunct—taxes are not levied against them; perhaps, you have more freedom to treat your place as your own.

Neither the original survey nor the later revision mark the fence surrounding the shack. According to both plottings, the shack's empty square sits close to Wendenworth Road near the place where the property my uncle calls "Herbst's hunter's" meets the property owned by H.'s Construction of San Antonio. By official cartographic reckoning, my family's country place doesn't even exist.

A year after my return to the Syring family, Uncle Herbert has decided to move north to Nebraska. His brother Uncle Benny has lived in Nebraska since he got out of the Marines more than twenty years ago, and now there seems to be something of a shift of place going on in my family.

It feels tectonic. Vast plates of family bodies and memories moving north, scattering far from what has been home. Uncle Joe moved to Nebraska after his divorce a year ago. Uncle Herbert plans to move there to help with H & B's, a Texas-style barbecue restaurant he and Uncle Benny own together, and to get a less physically demanding job—he's recently had colon and hernia surgery and may not be capable of maintaining full capacity as a fire fighter. Aunt Barbara and her daughter, Dawn, have already moved to Nebraska so Dawn can finish high school there rather than face the math portion of Texas' standardized tests for graduation. For a few months, I will be living with Uncle Herbert in his trailer house, helping him get ready for the move, and hearing more stories.

One night we sat together looking at the topographic maps for the area around the shack. At supper we'd been talking about some of the things scattered around his property, especially the old pieces of farm equipment that he bought from Theckla Wendenworth, the woman who lived down the road from the Syrings at the country place, when she sold her property on Curry Creek. We also talked about some old license plates he'd taken from inside Uncle Alfred's "new house." Aunt Frieda sold off much of the old equipment after Uncle Alfred died, and Uncle Herbert had been disappointed that she'd not given family members first opportunity to buy.

"You're the history keeper of the family, aren't you?" I said.

"I would imagine so. I don't know if others remember or not."

"I mean, not only the stories, but also the material things of the past. They're important to you."

"I guess they are, because I'd have liked to have his corn sheller that we shelled with, and the grinder. Some guy bid so much money to buy all the buildings after Uncle Alfred passed on, Aunt Frieda sold all the buildings. I just wandered in there when this guy was moving all this shit out, and I didn't realize that they weren't going to let the family come in and get an opportunity to get some of that old stuff. Old wooden wheelbarrow that Uncle Alfred and them built. And that guy was really going after that stuff."

"Why? What was he going to do with it?"

"Sell it . . . antiques. Oh, yes! a lot of antiques in that building. I got a little set of baby buggy wheels that were dad's. I got them, and they're up in the restaurant now, laying across the old apple box I found there. And he gave me a couple rusted out license plates, but he wanted to keep the old ones. I asked if I could go up in those walls [in one of the old buildings], tear them out. He sent another guy up there with me to evaluate them. He tore out one plate and looked at it and said I could go ahead and tear them all out. And then he wanted me to bring all those plates down there and let him go through them, so he could take any duplicates. I hid all the oldest ones . . . I told him 'All I got is late models.' I wasn't going to give him that 1936 model license plate I tore off that wall! I worked quite hard to get them off. He was buying the buildings for what was in them, not for the buildings themselves. And he wanted to take those plates, too, that greedy bastard."

"Where was this guy from?"

"Hell, I don't know. Some damn guy that Freddy Lux [a neighbor] knew. He was taking our history, Syring history, and selling it for a dollar. I took it and made license plates . . . framed them and put them in the restaurant. But he was going to just sell them to the highest bidder I would imagine. He was getting all those old Model T parts."

"I guess I understand why there's a distinction between this guy coming to take this stuff and you taking it, but tell me what you see as the difference between you framing the license plates, and him taking them and selling them."

"Because to the person that he would sell them to, I guess the history's not behind it. They were once on vehicles that were in the Syring family. To somebody else they would just be a license plate, a collector's item. To us, that's history . . . that's . . . those license plates used to be on one of our vehicles at one time. Just like that Model T, I hated to see that go when Dad sold it. 1928 Model T that his dad bought new in 1928. And my dad bought it for ten dollars in 1952 or '53 for the family. And we used to drive it. Your father Nicklaus drove it. And I drove it. It had a hard rubber wheel on one side, and the wooden spokes broke out on the other side, so Daddy had a steel wheel put on it. It looked weird, but we still had it. The spokes in front were metal, they were no longer wood. And we drove that Model T. Even back then somebody stole the cap off it because it was a collector's item. But to us that was important, that old Model T. Leaked oil like a sieve. We had a can tied to the side where it would drain out. Daddy'd take the can after it'd get 'bout half full and pour it back into the crankcase."

"So it would drain into the can and you'd just recycle it?"

"Yeah. Pour it back in there!" He laughs.

"One of the things I've noticed in all these stories is the way that everything is slapped together, made do, but everything is used and re-used again. You still do that. I mean, when we were picking up things out here to take to your place in Nixon, I said to the kid helping me— you were off somewhere, and we were picking up that metal stuff that was in the dirt and throwing it into buckets—I said, 'This guy doesn't throw anything away.'"

More laughter.

"Corby looked at me, he didn't say anything, but I thought his look was saying, 'Of course not. This stuff was useable once, and it may be useable again. We don't *know* what it will be useable for, but it will work.' He didn't say any of that, but the next day when we were on our way to Nixon, I said the same thing about not throwing stuff away to Richard [another teenager who is helping Uncle Herbert get ready to move to Nebraska]. Richard's a lot sharper, a lot more articulate, and he said exactly that: 'Well, you know, these things will be useful again.'"

"Yeah, it does become useful, you never know. That's why I never throw anything away. Barbara gets so mad at me, because . . . I guess the Syrings are that way. Uncle Alfred was too. You ought to see that big old metal pile I got down there. Well, you see that big old trailer I got parked next to the house. That metal all came off that Wendenworth place. And I picked it all up because I promised her I would clean the place up, but I also picked it up because I think I could use it."

"And you still think you can?"

"I've used some of it already! I use a piece of metal here and a piece there. I had a big heavy shaft, I was so disappointed, I had it on the back of my trailer, and I lost it on my way home one day. I was just sick that I lost that square shaft. And that had a lot of antique value, a lot of sentimental value, an old shaft from a horse wagon. I've always saved stuff. Up to the restaurant—that old double singletree, that came off that old Wendenworth place."

"Tell me why your taking stuff from the Wendenworth place and doing things with it is different than the guy coming and buying those plates and selling them?"

"Because that's my relatives. That's history. We helped make that history. I worked for them. And my dad and them were cousins, so I felt that it was still coming to a member of the family. I'd rather pass it on. I don't mind selling it to the family, but you know, then I know where it's going. The reason I went for that old equipment wasn't just the antiquish value, but realizing what kind of history went behind it. And her telling me how she worked with that equipment when it was bought. And that meant a lot to me, and now I've got a piece of that pie."

"What do you think about the people who come in, like from San Antonio, come in to these antique shops—not the guy that bought this stuff and resold it, but the people who actually come in and buy this stuff and take it home to decorate their houses—what do you think is going on there? Why do they want that stuff?"

"I think that they're doing the same thing I'm doing, they want to take a giant step backwards. They want to . . . if they knew the history behind it, it would be more valuable to them than just a decorator piece. I guess if you could understand the history behind it, it would be much more valuable."

"So that, basically, what you think is missing from those people's purchases is the stories?"

"The stories. The stories behind that wooden chair. That apple crate box that's been restored. That baby buggy. That old doll."

"Knowing who slept in that baby buggy. Or who used the wheels to make into a 'whee wheeler' for a tool and a toy."

"Yeah. See, the whee wheeler itself probably has very little value to somebody else. Probably ten dollars a wheel you could buy those wheels, but it means something else to me and brother Ben, probably Arthur, because we were the ones that built it, and used it for four or five years up the country. Getting wood in, getting deer in, getting anything that required a distance to move it. And it was important to have that whee wheeler. And we were so impressed with what we could build, and that it stayed together all these years."

But the old place, the home place, the family place hasn't held together. Many families in the Hill Country and elsewhere experience this dissipation of the energy that holds communities together, a sort of entropy of place. Lawrence Goodwyn quotes a Fredericksburg gunsmith:

> Some of us when we look around at what is happening, we feel we
> are losing ourselves. Outsiders are taking over. It's not all bad; they
> are good people by and large, and they help protect our buildings, and

bring money to the community, but the values are all different now. We used to be a town that didn't believe in easy money. There was a sense that an "honest day's work" got an "honest day's wages" and things had real value. I can't tell you exactly what that means, but I know it doesn't mean one more antique store selling what we used to live with. (Watriss and Baldwin 1991, 39)

This is a common enough story in the Hill Country, and in other rural places; I've heard versions of it from people I've met in Texas, Oregon, Iowa, Nebraska, Wisconsin, and Minnesota. In my family's case, the result of this separation from place and proximity to each other is a strong current of longing that is both exacerbated and alleviated through memory, storytelling, and fiercely defending the boundaries that define the last two acres of "old place" land still owned by family members.

Despite geographical distance, the Syrings do continue to rely on each other for community in vital ways. When Uncle Herbert and Uncle Benny bought an old house in a small Nebraska town for the bottom-dollar price of $4,000, an entire flock of Syrings and adopted Syrings gathered to help repaint and repair the building. Uncle Herbert provided the paint and supplies and a big meal for everybody, and the Syring "community" provided the labor. Since that effort, the house has been occupied and is being purchased from Uncle Herbert and Uncle Benny by one of Uncle Benny's own children.

The circulation of children has also served to maintain and cement kinship networks in my family. In this respect, my family seems to be a "throwback" to an earlier time and cultural practice. Demographers and social historians of the family have noted that family mobility patterns were transformed in the post–World War II years, with individual nuclear families moving from place to place based on job-related opportunities. The Syring family's mobility is, almost without exception, kinship based.

One of the things that most intrigues me about the Syring family as a community is the way that the children are as mobile as their parents, moving from one household to another as need and opportunity arise. In an earlier section of this writing, "Notes on a Hog Butchering," I described the odd moment when Uncle Robert addresses three boys who are each considered his "sons." Biology is only one of the criteria for determining kinship. One "son," the biological offspring of Aunt Virginia, lived off and on with Uncle Robert and Aunt Schatze his entire life. Another was Robert's biological offspring from a previous marriage, and the third was Robert's adopted child from his wife's previous marriage.

This represents a kinship network made complex by child mobility and the formation and dissolution of various nuclear families. The result, while messy, multiplies the number of options available for children. I have used such kinship networks and opportunities in my own life. Though I am focusing in this writing on the Syring (my father's) side of the family, my mother's family carries some similar characteristics. Coming from immigrant backgrounds in which the move to the United States was facilitated by family connections, both my mother's parents understood the need for extended kinship support. Their children (my mother and her sisters) acquired such an understanding of the role of kin as well, and when, at fifteen, I asserted my own need for an "outlet" from the emotional and psychic wreck of my parents' relationship, when I needed to escape from the closed world of a mobile and isolated nuclear family, I spent my high school years living with my mother's sister, Jean, and her family. Jean's family already included three children who were technically her niece and nephews. Rather than let the children be sent away from their own kin, Jean and her husband adopted the children of her sister Marty, after Aunt Marty died of a brain tumor in the 1960s.

Such extension of family appears to be undergoing a shift in availability in my own generation as the grandchildren of Opa Ben and Oma Aurelia scatter geographically and, more importantly, experientially. Unlike the large nucleus of thirteen people who grew up under similar conditions and experiences, the Syrings of my generation have divergent memories of childhood. Perhaps the only thing my generation has in common is the experience of growing up in families that fit within the definition of "impoverished" according to federal policymakers. This seems to be fragile grounds for fusing literal kinship into community.

Uncle Herbert, Aunt Virginia, Uncle Benny, and the rest constantly retell the stories of the life and times of the Syrings in the rural Hill Country to prevent this dissolution of family. It is a ritual means both of affirming the communal aspect of their own pasts and of trying to convey that experience, even with its deprivation and abuses, to their own children so that they might share in the collective entity known as "the Syrings."

In a sense, these stories form a site for re-creating the family. While the subject matter of these stories might be "in the past," and therefore subject to dismissal as uncritical "nostalgia," the intended effect of these narrations is in the present—that is, to identify the threads that connect the Syring community to one another and to include multiple generations in a collective ritual. What actually happened in the past, in those places, is less important than the fact that those things are remembered, retold, and revalued in the current moment. While the stories are in the past, it is the cultural moment of the telling of the story that binds the Syring family together, holds my attention, brings me "home," and absorbs me in a questioning of the role of family, storytelling, and nostalgia.

Fences—Contested Goatpaths and Gates

But the new prosperity has a price. In the 1970s, as wealthy newcomers began to buy the Edwards Plateau and preserve it, they began to appropriate it and, inevitably, to define it. . . . Coincident with the rebirth of interest in ethnic history and the search for "roots" in the late 1960s and 1970s, urban wealth began to move out of Dallas and Houston, Austin and San Antonio into the Hill Country. The things that had made life so difficult for so long turned out to be the very things that, in preserving the land, have made it so attractive to outsiders.

Lawrence Goodwyn, *Coming to Terms:
The German Hill Country of Texas*

Grasses and broadleaf plants coexist closely by sharing light and soil nutrients at different levels and different times of the year; in spite of relentlessly fierce competition, species so balance themselves that a big increase of one at the expense of others hardly happens unless there is outside disturbance. In mature grassland the communities are diversely full yet in equilibrium, but I haven't heard of any prairie politician seeing or caring to apply the parable.

William Least Heat-Moon, *Prairyerth: A Deep Map*

The big problem that fences cope with—or are supposed to—is of course most domesticated animals' flat distaste for staying where you want them to be. True, some fences are erected to keep people in or out of certain premises, but they are fairly useless for this purpose unless backed by armed might, as East Berlin wall guards could tell you, or any small-rancher in deer-hunting country.

John Graves, *From a Limestone Ledge*

Fences are particularly on Uncle Herbert's mind lately. Moving a small bit of fence a few feet is one of the most important projects he has to complete before he leaves for Nebraska in May. The property including the shack is not large but the wealthy San Antonio businessman who currently owns the neighboring property, which used to be the Syring homestead, wants to make it even smaller. He recently had his sheep-hand put in a new fence, and in the process, took a 125-foot-by-15-foot piece of my uncle's property for his own. The story as Uncle Herbert tells it goes like this:

"See, K. [I will use an initial to represent the businessman while maintaining his anonymity] put his fence in on this old right of way that we had put in for Uncle Alfred."

"He thought it was his property?"

"Yeah, he thought it was his because it was on the map, but that right of way was put in by my father and Uncle Alfred. It was a gentle-man's agreement. Uncle Alfred sold my daddy that land and the condi-tion was that he would have a right of way to run his goats. He was afraid they wouldn't go around to the other side of our property. So they put in that right of way, but Uncle Alfred never used it. Never had any problems getting the goats out around the other side."

"So the right of way was just that narrow part with openings on ei-ther end, and Opa Ben owned it?"

"We owned it, and the surveyors say we still do. The surveyor came out and found the stake on that corner, and it shows that the right of way belongs to us, not K. We gave Uncle Alfred the use of the right of way, but there was never anything in writing."

"Did you say that to K.?"

"I sent him two letters. Had my lawyer help me write them."

"Did K. answer them?"

"The first one he answered. He said that the piece was his and he wasn't going to move the fence."

"And the second letter?"

"No answer. I guess he figures I won't have the money to sue him, and if he has the property for a few years and can prove that he made improvements on it, which is what the fence would be called, then it will become his by law."

"So what's going to happen?"

"I'm going to move that fence myself. I can't let it wait until after I move because I may not get a chance to come back down very soon. And I'll tell you, that gate that he's put in on our property will not be staying there. So I've got to move it before I leave, then if he wants it to become a court thing, he'll have to sue me instead."

When you walk out the gate in front of the shack the first thing you see is the Burn across the road. Uncle Herbert says his father and Uncle Alfred burned off that pastureland long before 1957 when Opa Ben moved his family up here to live. The cedar brakes were burned off in an attempt to restore the balance between trees and grass that existed on this slope long ago. The Burn is mostly open grass and a few scattered oaks where there used to be nothing but dense stands of cedars. The deer like to skirt its edges and browse the shrubby plants which grow well there.

The deer in the Hill Country probably outnumber the people now. This is a result of two processes. First, the number of predators has severely declined in the last one hundred fifty years—the only predatory worries the deer have now is during two months of hunting season beginning in November, and occasional poachers, like my family, who sometimes take a deer out of season. The second process that has led to the predominance of four-legged ungulates in the Hill Country is the flow of people to urban spaces. "Natives" who care for and depend on the land for a living are almost as scarce as the Comanches and Tonkawa and the wolves, bears, and cougars that used to control the deer population.

There are exceptions, of course. Fredericksburg, with its continuous streams of tourists like trout to be plucked from a river and drained of their surplus moneys, prospers today more than it ever did. But places like Stonewall, Comfort, Kendalia, and the Burn sit largely unoccupied, buildings eventually to be sold to a city person seeking a country hideaway. Once when I commented to Uncle Herbert that a lot of the property surrounding his small holding in rural Comal County was for sale, he said: "All the land around here is for sale if somebody makes a decent offer." A newspaper in Boerne claims Kendall County, where the shack sits, is the fastest-growing county in Texas.

Until last spring the Burn was unfenced, an expanse of sunburned bluestem, side oats and grama grasses, limestone, and opuntia cacti stretching from the shack down to the marshy place my family calls "the Slash." I could walk out the gate and into hundreds of acres of ground that nobody had used, or abused, for decades. Last year somebody from San Antonio bought the property and decided to run a few goats on it. The fence they put up is made of taut wire and creosote-soaked posts hauled in from somewhere else. They could have saved the money and used cedar from the hills around here.

Now I walk down toward Curry Creek between parallel metal wire barriers that break up the landscape like webs. The walk seems longer now, though I know the actual distance remains the same. The armadillos still move in the brush on either side, and sometimes I can see them rush across the bare surface of the road. Why did the armadillo cross the road? To squeeze through the fence on the other side.

The fence surrounding the shack is sagging. For a while I thought about asking my uncle whether he wanted me to bring a few of his goats up for a summer season dining on grass ungrazed for years. But my uncle sold all of his goats recently, to prepare for his move up to Nebraska, so the issue has fallen into the possible pasts. Now I stay up here alone with the armadillos. Undoubtedly this is for the best since I would otherwise have to fix the fence.

The grasses don't care about dilapidated fences. The Hill Country isn't really part of a prairie, though below the Balcones Escarpment, the eastern boundary of the region, some of the most fertile prairie lands of Texas gather the runoff from Hill Country springs and rivers. Prairie grasses grow here too. Before 1860, prior to the rapid settlement of the area by Europeans, the area that now makes up Kendall County has been estimated to have been about half grasslands and half wooded.

Grasses still grow here, though there has been a clear shift from the longer grasses to intermediate and short grasses as overgrazing has wiped out the tallgrass communities. Once the Hill Country supported a community that included big bluestem, little bluestem, and Indian grass, the long-bearded mainstays of the true (tallgrass) prairies that once swept up the middle of North America from Texas to Canada. Now even in moderately grazed areas scarce patches of the shorter variety of bluestem mix with Texas wintergrass, white tridens, Texas cup grass, tall dropseed, side oats grama, seep muhly, and common curly mesquite. In heavily grazed areas, curly mesquite assumes dominance along with three-awn, Texas grama, red grama, hairy grama, hairy tridens, and white tridens. Cedar sage and cedar brakes expand into these grasslands and continue the process of fragmenting the prairies that began with the breaking of prairie soils by pioneer plows.

The Burn has been a source of good hunting for my family for years. Uncle Herbert tells a story about a time when he went hunting up there with several of my other uncles. They all picked a corner and just waited for the deer to come to them. Uncle Herbert sat in his van with one of my cousins and watched across the road into the (then unfenced) Burn, and he was the only one to even see a deer on that trip. He shot two in quick succession, while nobody else got anything. The family still laughs about Uncle Joe traveling nearly a thousand miles from Nebraska just to watch Uncle Herbert shoot deer.

But those opportunities are over; the new fence extends too high to lift out a deer, and the gate remains solidly padlocked. Syrings won't be able to shoot into the Burn for deer anymore. There is nothing tragic in this; in fact, shooting a deer on somebody else's property clearly offered legal obstacles prior to the building of that fence, but I can't help feeling a change in the order of the world is registered in those strands of barbed wire.

For several years, the children of Opa Ben depended on the good will of neighbors and the leniency of the local game warden in order to feed themselves with deer, jackrabbit, squirrel, wild turkey, and whatever other game the land offered. Even then, shooting deer out of season was illegal, but the local knowledge of need tempered the application of the law. Like grasses and broadleaf plants in equilibrium, Opa Ben's family used hunting to coexist with the people who had more substantial landholdings and financial resources.

Today the surrounding properties are mostly owned by people who don't live up here. Much of the land enclosing the shack's few acres has been bought by a businessman who lives in San Antonio. In the time I've been staying at the shack, I've never seen the owner come by on his way down to the old Syring house that is now the center of his property.

He's hired a Mexican sheephand to tend the animals and build fence. I only know this because I walked over the hill to the old place and went inside. It looks run down and when nobody answered my knock, I walked inside to see the rooms where my great-uncles, great-aunts, and grandfather lived. I'd been in that house a few times when I was young, but remembered very little about it.

The house was nearly empty. A refrigerator in the kitchen. An old table. The refrigerator was running. It was full of beer and the freezer had a few pounds of hamburger, some deer steaks, and that was all. In what used to be the living room, I found two cots, and a notebook with a name, Alberto Ortiz, written in a young child's handwriting, a pile of change on the windowsill, and I realized I was trespassing. Somebody lived there, and I was prying into their things. Evidence of the absence of community—I know nothing about the people who live in the place of my family's past, and here I am, intruding on their lives.

Symbiosis between people no longer seems to be the basis of life here. When I stayed at the shack the first time, I went down to a low-water crossing on the creek to fill my water container—the same place where my father often went swimming when he was young. While I kneeled in the stream gravel filling the orange cooler, two men stopped their pickup on the road, climbed out, and confronted me.

"What are you doing?" one asked while the other stood silently on the bank opposite me.

"I'm staying up the road on the old Syring place. It was my grandfather's, and my uncle owns it now. I just need some water to drink for the weekend," I said. The man seemed unimpressed by my explanation.

"You know you're on private property there. You can finish what you're doing now, but remember that trespassing is an arrestable offense," he concluded, and the two of them climbed back into their truck and drove away.

When I left after the weekend I saw that yet another fence had been stretched across the stream alongside the crossing. (Recently, when I went up to the country place with my uncle, the fence was gone again, washed out by a heavy winter rainstorm.)

My uncle explains that tourism has become a problem in the Hill Country. People who come out for weekend parties or explorations often trespass and knock down fences, destroy pasture grasses, and leave litter, some of which can be costly to a rancher. His own milk cow died last year from a distended stomach, the result of eating plastic garbage bags that had been tossed on the roadside.

A column in the Fredericksburg newspaper points to the primary concern for landowners:

> Throughout the year, the Loop [a nearby rural route] is taken by both local and visitor alike to get a good gulp of the outdoors. However, because of ignorance of landowners' rights or perhaps an overaggressive public wanting a closer look, people have tromped all over the place.
>
> While the damage done to private property may be negligible, there is cause for concern. Certainly the liability question comes foremost to mind. An accident or snake bite could result in a civil suit. (*Standard-Radio Post*, March 17, 1993)

When a woman relative of mine was bitten by a rattlesnake at the beginning of the twentieth century, the family that owned the property where she was bitten offered their condolences at the funeral. At the end of this century, the expected response to walking in ignorance into dangers inherent in the landscape is a lawsuit. To apply the parable in the quotation at the beginning of this section: the community of grasses (long-time residents) and broadleaf plants (newcomers) couldn't be further from equilibrium.

On the Devil's Backbone—Changing Places

> Most scholars agree that relocation involves short-term disruptions that can be stressful. Although a fairly frequent event, with one in five moving yearly, U.S. samples have rated relocation as a fairly stressful event. Nevertheless, there are ways of experiencing the move that make it more manageable.
>
> Barbara Brown and Douglas Perkins, "Disruptions in
> Place Attachment," in *Place Attachment*

After a last few days of hurried packing and loading of trailers, my uncle leaves for Nebraska in the morning. Tonight, after helping with the final preparations, I am driving toward the shack along a stretch of State Highway 32 locally known as "The Devil's Backbone." Sharp ups and downs, narrow ridgetops, precipitous slopes on either side giving way to broad views of spring green valleys—during the day this place seems to offer glimpses of a prototype of heaven as much as flashes of diabolic terror.

Once when my father drove along this road late at night under a full moon, I remember lying in the back of a pickup truck with one of my sisters and feeling simultaneously terrified and exhilarated as the moon-lit landscape fell away into the distances on either side of the road. My father has been a professional tractor-trailer driver for years, but that night I think he had been drinking and playing music, and the terror was very real as he took curves like a racecar driver—driving in the opposing lane to reduce the corner, a technique my uncle calls "cutting the cabbage."

Tonight I drive slowly, taking in the pinpoints of light in the valleys and mulling over what I feel. On the seat beside me are three wooden cutouts in the shape of armadillos. During the packing, we came upon a box full of wooden things made by Opa Ben and salted away like dried sausage to be eaten later. One of the cutouts was already painted, its claws, tail, and the nine bands across its back painted white and black with a gray body. Uncle Herbert gave me the painted one, and I asked him for two of the unfinished ones to complete myself.

There were also three or four of the simple wood crosses my grandfather made late in his life to give to his family members. Uncle Herbert offered one of these to me as well, but I declined, choosing not to invite into my life whatever ambiguous faith Opa Ben might have harbored in his hard heart.

I stop at a bar called The Devil's Backbone Place to think about what my uncle's move means—to him, to the family, to myself. The Place is nearly empty; I've never been here before. A few men sit at a table watching the last fifteen minutes of the final episode of the television series *Cheers*. The woman tending the bar returns to her stool to watch after she places a single shot of whiskey on the counter in front of me. I have not seen this program in years, but, impossibly, it seems to be about saying "goodbye to a place."

This evening, after we had finished loading the heavy furniture, Uncle Herbert took all of us—the people who had helped him over the past few months—to dinner. "You've all been working for me, so it's time that I work a little for all of you," he said before we drove to an "all-you-can-eat" restaurant.

After a brief thanksgiving and prayer for a safe trip, we all wandered off to gather food from the huge "wonder-bar" loaded with salads, potatoes, and meat. Since Uncle Herbert is moving to work in the restaurant he owns with Uncle Benny, it seems appropriate that this "closing ritual" take place in a public eating place.

Uncle Herbert is the last of my immediate clan of Syrings to live in the rural spaces of the Hill Country. All of my aunts and uncles have moved to New Braunfels, San Antonio, Houston, as far west as El Paso, and as far north as Nebraska. The scattering of place has been completed, and we are all, strictly speaking, rootless now.

While we packed, I asked Uncle Jerry if he thought Uncle Herbert would carry out his plan to live in Nebraska for fifteen years and then retire to some property he is buying near Nixon, Texas.

"So much stuff to move," I said. "I can't imagine that after fifteen years he will want to go through this all over again in order to return south."

"You just don't know with Herbie," Uncle Jerry said. "If he sets his mind to it, then he'll probably do it. He's already built that shed down there in Nixon. I imagine he'll come back and build him a house there."

Uncle Herbert has also planted four pecan saplings at the Nixon place, and I've agreed to make a few trips down there to water them through the summer. Uncle Herbert says if they make it through the first year, they'll do fine because by next year, they will have set down their deep taproots. "For the first year or two, pecans grow downward," he told me once. "It won't look like they're growing much, but they are getting themselves rooted. Then they'll shoot up." So, I'm the pecan support crew now.

Is this the best model of rootedness I can find? To plant a few pecans in hopes of future return? And these in the flatlands below the region that represents "home" in all these family stories.

I have already set up a new home in Fredericksburg, a move I made a month ago so I would have a place to stay after Uncle Herbert left. The brief time during which I lived with him in his partially packed mobile home lasted only a few months. He jokes that I abandoned him. There is a seriousness inside that joke, and I suppose I left early as much to avoid feeling abandoned myself as to get established in a new place.

When I arrived yesterday to help pack, Uncle Herbert showed me a videotape of the farmhouse Aunt Barbara had found for them in Nebraska. They are going to buy the house and half a dozen outbuildings on five acres for $40,000, a figure that Uncle Benny said was $10,000 too high.

"He's been living there too long," Uncle Herbert said. "He's become tight like all those other damn Bohemian farmers up there." We both laughed. "They want to get things given to them."

Uncle Herbert and Aunt Barbara will move into that house and work with Uncle Benny and his wife, Jean, to try to turn H & B's Texas Style Bar-B-Q into a success in the middle of Nebraska corn and alfalfa fields. They have already begun the process of making a new place for themselves.

I look up at the television, which has switched from the sitcom to news of the end of the Spurs' basketball season, and I am the only one left in the bar with the bartender.

"Want another?" she asks, but I've already set the empty shotglass of Seagram's Seven on the counter, and turned to the door to drive along the Devil's Backbone to spend the night at the shack.

Riding the Devil's Spine

Tonight I drive the stretch of road called the Devil's Backbone, and think of the story you told about that bottle of whiskey you stole with your brothers. "Memories," you said and laughed. Those memories make my blood jump now, years later, on a road you'd never heard of when you first drank. I watched you lower that bottle, now nearly empty, into a box, and I knew something had closed—something as simple and se-cret as the life of a place.

I arrive at the place I call "the shack," which makes you laugh be-cause you call it, "the country place"—it is the difference between you who lived here once and I who visit here only briefly. Tired with pack-ing your belongings, I lower myself to sleep on the floor of the old smokehouse.

Sometime before dawn, I climb into my truck. The sheep are bawl-ing in the next pasture over. I'm heading toward my new home. May we someday both find the place where the whiskey water waits for every-thing under the earth—the roots of your pecans and my garden, and both our tongues, thirsty for more stories.

St. Joseph's Church, Honey Creek, built in 1912 to replace an earlier log and rock church.

Part 2

Honey Creek Church

CHAPTER AND VERSE

Here I am, where I ought to be.

A writer must have a place where he or she feels this, a place to love and be irritated with. One must experience the local blights, hear the proverbs, endure the radio commercials, go to reservation churches, roundhouses, cafes, and bingo palaces. By the close study of a place, its people and character, its crops, products, paranoias, dialects, and failures, we come closer to our reality. It is difficult to impose a story and a plot on a place. However, truly knowing a place forms the suggestive basis for every kind of linking circumstance. Location, whether it is to abandon it or draw it sharply, is where we start.

Louise Erdrich, "A Writer's Sense of Place,"
in *A Place of Sense: Essays in Search of the Midwest*

There are places around which the lives and imaginations of families and entire communities can revolve. The Laubach House, the country place (what I call the shack), and especially Honey Creek Church are some of these such places for my family. For at least four generations before me—my great-great grandparents, my great-grandparents, my grand-parents, and my father and uncles and aunts—Honey Creek Church and its attendant burying ground has been a point of preoccupation. The Scheel family cemetery on the old Scheel place was disinterred and moved to Honey Creek after the property was sold. Gross-Oma and Gross-Opa Scheel, whom I remember first as a wrinkled-necked, thin couple living in San Antonio in a house that smelled like sausage frying and then as an old widower hauled to family events in a wheelchair and parked like a car by the door, are buried at the church, though they'd lived out of country for years before they died. My father's parents are buried there, with a murky cameo-shaped photograph of their wedding (in the same church) held in a plate on their joint tombstone. I remember that my father and mother fought over where they, and therefore their chil-dren, were to lie after death. My mother wanted to return to Nebraska, where her own youth, family, and memories lay, and my father, insisting on the inexorability of history, named St. Joseph's at Honey Creek as his final place. I believe he even tried to purchase several grave plots, though he couldn't afford them at the time.

Walker Percy wrote, "Places aren't so much occupied anymore, as they are consumed, used up, by people living modern lives." Some places, however, still accrue meaning over time, rather than becoming drained of it. For my family, Honey Creek Church contains a surfeit of mean-ing, far beyond what even the prodigious Syring appetite will ever be able to consume.

The church and its environs have history on their side for my fam-ily. There's also memory—the memory of the few years my father and his brothers and sisters lived with their parents in "the Laubach Place," a ramshackle house set back in the live oaks, maybe a hundred yards from the door of St. Joseph's. Many stories rise out of the five or six rooms of that house and sit squarely in my family's memory to this day. The time Nicklaus broke the radio that was supposed to be sacred prop-erty hauled down only to listen to oompah music out of New Braunfels on Sunday evenings. The time the Mexican guy came up the road looking for a little food in return for work and was run off by my grandfather with a shotgun. The way my grandmother kept chickens in the cellar. The way Syrings acquired their reputation as "wreckas" because the kids broke everything, including the fine old carriage that hung in the garage and had belonged to the Laubachs. The kids hauled it down and turned it into a sort of downhill racer, a brief-lived but glorious children's toy.

So Honey Creek is where the heart is, at least the imaginative heart of my family. Even the Syrings of my own generation, in their financial strugglings and urban lives, get swept up in the stories told by our parents about the places in the hills where we still go for family reunions, funerals, and Easter visits.

Father Bonnie and His Flock

1980 (1916)

Father Ewald Bonifacious stepped down the stone pathway and made his way to the first station of the cross. The women who had gathered for this Easter walk followed closely behind, and though this was supposed to be a solemn occasion, the old priest couldn't help but think of the children's game, follow-the-leader. He'd been playing that game himself the first time he'd entered into the mystery of the calling that had claimed him for most of his seventy years.

"Come on, Bonnie, it's in the rules!" his older brother, Benedictus Jerome, yelled from the steps of the old Honey Creek Church. "You got to go where the leader goes, else you lose."

Aurelia and Genevieve Agnes had already gone inside the church—Genevieve Agnes was the leader and she never feared anything. No threat of punishment or reprisal could deter Agnes when she got a notion into her head, and her current idea was to lead the way into the church to see whether they might be able to steal some of the sacramental wine. Not enough to get drunk or anything, but enough to test whether any of her brothers or her sister was as brave as she was. She wanted to see whether they'd flirt with damnation.

Bennie disappeared, and Ewald watched with mixed emotions as the wooden door closed. If he didn't go in, he would lose the game, and be called a chicken for days, too. But if he did go in, he would be going against his parents' orders and risk transgressing a higher authority as well. It was then that he had his first vision.

"You are always welcome in my Father's house." The voice came from a bearded man wearing sandals and a robe. One moment Ewald was alone with the hot sun baking his bare head, and the next, he was in the shadow of this stranger. "Go in, child. Rest in the coolness of my Father's house." And without thinking, Ewald pulled open the door and went into the dimness. After a moment his eyes adjusted, and he saw his sisters and his brother standing behind the altar, trying to open the sacristy to get at the wine. They all three looked startled since they expected Ewald to be one of their parents or the priest. Ewald usually refused to follow them into illicit territory.

"Bonnie!" the three of them shrieked in unison, and they all started giggling.

"Well, we're a whole damned family now!" Agnes delightedly screamed.

Ewald felt calm and clear-headed.

"Forgive them, Father; they don't know what they're doing," he mumbled at the same time that Benedictus got the sacristy open.

"What's that?" Agnes said to Ewald. "You thinking you're Jesus or something, now, Bonnie?" They all three laughed again. "Our Bonnie, who art in heaven, hollow be thy name," Benedictus added. "You can't be Jesus," Agnes concluded. "You got too many brothers and sisters for that."

Ewald sat down in the back pew and looked around while the three of them took turns sipping from the wine flask. It was cool inside the church, just like the man outside had said. He'd been inside the church many times with his family, but never when the building was empty. Even with his siblings laughing and goofing around at the church's front, the building seemed grandly peaceful. It felt like being inside the body of a very big fish, with the ceiling beams curving up like ribs to meet at the peak.

"God is a fish," Ewald thought to himself. "A fish that has already eaten each and every one of us, even if we don't know it."

While Ewald sat there quietly contemplating the implications of his novel conception of God, the church door opened suddenly, and their mother, Laura, swirled in the door like a broody hen descending on a rat in the chicken house.

"I'm gonna tan each and every inch of each and every one a your tails," she hollered as she stormed up the aisle. While she walked, she made the sign of the cross with the hand she had, by force of habit, dipped in the basin of holy water beside the door. She swept right past Ewald without actually seeing him, and that, to Ewald Bonifacious, was enough miracle to prove the existence of God. Laura's mastery of switching her children without breaking skin was legendary, and any opportunity to avoid a whipping at her hands was reason to believe. Ewald slipped out the door and ran to the graveyard where the children were supposed to have been working to weed the family's grave plots. He ran past the graves of his grandparents and hurried on to the top end of the cemetery where various Scheels, Hildebrandts, Friesenhahns, and Weidners were buried. He figured his mother had heard the voices of his brother and sisters as she passed the church and not even bothered to look at the upper end of the graveyard. He quickly set to, pulling sprouting dandelions and devil's claws from the grave of Mathilda Kuntz, recently deceased.

"Bonifacious!" he heard his mother call from the church steps, but he could tell by her voice that she wasn't angry at him. He almost never joined the other children in their worst mischief, so she had no reason to suspect her youngest son had been inside the church too. He also knew that despite their teasing of him, his sisters and brothers would abide by the strict code of honor that precluded tattling on one another under any circumstances. They all knew that Ewald had never tattled on them for anything, though he could have many times over.

He hurried down the hill to where his mother waited, his sisters and brother wailing and red-faced beside her. She had not whipped them yet, since such a thing would be inappropriate in the house of the Lord, but they knew that when they got home, the smell of the Lord's blood still on their breaths, they were going to be pounded until they wished they were buried in the cemetery themselves. Ewald felt sad that they would suffer, but he did not speak up and add his own name to the list of kids to be switched. After all, he had been invited into the church by the Son himself.

Father Bonifacious genuflected at the next station—Christ falls for the first time—and all of the women following him knelt too. He couldn't shake the feeling. Follow-the-leader. Where was he going to take them this time?

One of the women, Jenny Ellen Neugebauer, fell to the ground. She was always the first to be slain in the spirit. She crumpled into the cedar bark shavings of the trail as if she were carrying Our Lord's Burden herself, and for the first time in his years of priesthood, Ewald Bonifacious had to stifle an urge to laugh. Jenny Ellen looked like a red-headed rag doll carelessly tossed aside by a bored child. Her dress had fluffed indecorously up and exposed a white thigh to the morning light. She was breathing deeply and, once again, dramatically proving her faith in front of the Lord and everybody.

The Time We Had All Those Watermelons

1956

The time we had all those watermelons was when this Mexican guy came looking for something to eat. Daddy was giving us all haircuts on the side of the house, and we were sitting there along the edge of the porch like a line of people on a pew at mass. The girls were all getting shingle-bobs—straight across the front, and then dropped down below their ears. Looked like Daddy put a bowl on their heads, but he didn't. The boys all got peeled onion cuts, right down to the skin. That way it'd always look good, Daddy said. Wouldn't have to worry about the lice, and it would always look the same. It wasn't until later that I thought about that and realized that always looking the same isn't exactly the same thing as always looking good.

But right then it felt like a party, all of us waiting our turns, and thinking about all those watermelons inside, rolled under the beds and waiting for Daddy to cut them up into green and red slices, like juicy smiles. He got them real cheap the day before. He drove down to San Antonio, to that big vegetable market they got down there, and late in the day he was able to get all those watermelons, enough to fill the whole backseat—at least where the backseat would have been if it had one—of the old Ford somebody'd given us. He got home late, so we were all asleep, but he woke us up anyway, and made us carry all those watermelons into the house and roll them away under the beds. We didn't count them, but I know that I carried at least six or seven, and there were twelve of us kids, then, that were big enough to carry, though I guess Magdalene didn't count since she only carried one, and that one she dropped. It fell in the dirt beside the porch and splattered into a sticky mess for the chickens and bugs to eat in the morning.

We were sitting there on the side porch and had either gotten, were getting, or were about to get our new haircuts, and then we were going to get to eat enough watermelon to make it come out our ears. Enough watermelon to make our bellies bloat. Enough watermelon to make us think that watermelon was all we would ever eat ever again.

That's when this Mexican guy came up the road. He must have heard us all hollering. Or smelled the charcoal kiln that we had going down by the tank. Cause you can't really see the house from the main road. The old stone church blocked that house from the road. We were living there behind that church because the owners knew how it could get rough with all those kids and no steady work, so they let Daddy and Mama and all us kids live there in return for taking care of the church-yard and cleaning the pastor's house and stuff.

So this Mexican guy comes up the little side road that ran by the church and up the hill toward the owner's house, and he kind of stops by the gate and looks at us. We weren't much to see, just a dozen dirty-faced kids and a fat man on a porch, but this Mexican guy looked at us like we was Jesus and the Apostles. He looked at us like we owned the end to all suffering. I remember he looked tired—and sunburned. He was so burnt he was almost black. The creases where his elbows bent, they were blue he was so black. He looked like he might of walked all the way from Mexico to where we lived.

This Mexican guy rubbed his stomach and said something like, "Tienes un pequito lunche?" And us kids thought, at least I did anyway, "God, you know! We can work this guy. Get him to do some of our work for us for a little lunch."

But Daddy, he never did like strangers, and he was prejudiced, I guess, too.

Daddy says to Nicklaus, my oldest brother, "Nick-laus, gehen haus und geholen meine Schrottlinte! Ich gibt ihn ein pequito lunche!"

So Nicklaus goes inside the house, and this Mexican guy, he looks relieved, I guess 'cause he was so hungry and he thought he was going to get some food finally. But when Nicklaus come out, he was carrying Daddy's old twelve-gauge, and that Mexican guy's eyes, they went just about round, like comic strip eyes, and he took off running across the pasture!

Now, I don't think Daddy would have shot him—there probably weren't even any shells in that shotgun, because Daddy never kept it loaded. But Daddy, like I said, he didn't like strangers, and he didn't want anybody, especially a Mexican, around with all those kids. He didn't want them around at all; he was very prejudiced.

So Daddy took that shotgun from my brother, and leaned it up against the porch post, and he went back to giving the rest of us our haircuts.

And when he was done, he told five or six of us to go on in the house and get some watermelons, and we all went in and tried to find the biggest ones we could lay our hands on while Daddy went into the kitchen and got the big butchering knife. Pretty soon we were all stuffing our mouths with juicy fruit, and spitting the seeds like buckshot at one another yelling, "Here you go, have a little lunch!"

Why Did the Shack Get Built?

1957

Ben sent two of his sons, Nicklaus and Herbert, over to Alfred Engel's place to borrow the old black pickup Alfred used to carry his groceries and feed. It was raining the day they started the move, but they went ahead anyway because Hermann Laubach said he needed the house behind the church for his daughter to live in since her husband had lost his job at the lime kiln in town. But Ben knew the Laubachs had another house his daughter could have moved into. Hermann wanted Ben out because his growing family of children were breaking everything in the place. Just like that, the Sürings were left without a house to sleep in.

Well, not exactly without a house altogether. Ben had been putting up a little one-room building down by the tank near the charcoal kilns. He told his children that the little house was for him to paint in, and for him and Aurelia to watch over the kilns at night, but the truth was that

Ben felt crowded. Too many children. Too many eyes and ears. The sounds of too many bodies breathing in the four rooms of the Laubach house.

Ben wanted space. He wanted rooms where if he walked in one direction, he could take a dozen long steps and not hit a wall or a body sleeping on the floor. Sometimes at night he would go down the little dirt road leading up to the house and walk over to the Honey Creek Church door. He liked the way the door felt heavy, substantial, as if the only hand strong enough to set it in place had been the Lord's himself. Ben wanted a door like that, and he wanted to put the pins in the hinges with his own thick fingers.

He would pull the door open and stand there watching the way the votive candles danced in their red glass holders, and he saw the way they filled the interior with mysterious light, the kind of light that had to belong to either a church or a whorehouse. That light promised fulfillment, spiritual or physical, and he would stand on the threshold enchanted by the promise, though he never felt like it was a promise meant for him. He wouldn't know what fulfillment looked like if it walked over and wrapped its arms around him.

But the candles were not the reason he always came back. He would go inside and close his eyes as he started up the aisle. The sensation of space overwhelmed him then—moving step by step through a space that was uncluttered and indoors. Huge spaces were common enough to him during the day. Sometimes he worked clearing trees for the power company. The sky loomed large around him. The dry hills had a way of stretching out into the distance as if they covered the whole planet, one cedar-scrubbed rise after another.

Inside the church was space contained, enough space to move around in, to breathe, and to hear nothing but the sound of candle wax sputtering and your own voice if you chose to speak. This was as close to heaven as Ben knew he would ever come.

When Hermann Laubach told Ben Süring he had to move, even the peace of those nighttime moments inside the church became something Ben couldn't have. They moved that one-room building up to country, and it became the seed that grew into the slapdash house where the Sürings lived.

The Mugging of Nicklaus

1959

It wasn't that Blackie and Shorty Weidner had any particular liking for Nicklaus Süring, but when you find a man unconscious and bleeding by the side of the road, to do anything less than stop in the middle of whatever errand you're running to give him your full aid and attention would be to make you accomplice to whatever circumstances got him knocked cold in the first place.

They were on their way to pick up some fencing supplies, and it was Blackie who saw Nicklaus Süring first. Blackie was sitting in the passenger's seat as they drove toward the store at Bergheim. They had just passed by St. Joseph's at Honey Creek, and Blackie was staring blankly out the window when he saw the body slumped in the ditch. They went by fast enough that at first he thought it was a deer lying there, which would have been cause enough to stop, since the meat might still be good if the kill were fresh. But then what he'd seen registered, and he realized it was a black-haired man stripped naked lying there. Nicklaus's skin was deeply tan, the brownish color of doeskin, so the mistake was an easy enough one to make at fifty miles an hour. Shorty swung into the entrance of the next ranch and turned back to the bridge.

Nicklaus lay in the ditch just below where the bridge started, not more than four or five feet from the current of the creek. Not until hours later, after they'd driven back to the rectory of the church where Father Bonifacious, the Sürings' uncle, was pastor and the doctor had driven out from Boerne, would the Weidner brothers have any idea how Nicklaus ended up there, beaten and robbed by those claiming to be his friends. But when they climbed down into the ditch, it looked as if the man had tried to take a skinny-dipping dive from the bridge and missed the water. Given Nicklaus Süring's history of drinking, it might have been the truth.

Blackie was the first to get down there in the rank grass of the ditch, and he found Nicklaus lying on his side in the midst of a patch of weeds. His skin was cool, and there was a fair amount of blood matted into his thick hair, but he was breathing evenly, surrounded by the smell of Indian blanket flowers and drying summer grasses.

Fattest Aunt

1981

We're waiting for the fattest aunt, the one whose dresses look big enough to make a circus tent when they hang out on the washline, and they've got bright patterns on them, too, like some kind of flowered sail. She's gone up to the top of the hill to walk around the path of our savior, which is a great place to mess around, but she won't let us go up there no more since she found us playing inside the little model of the sepulcher that they got set up at the last station.

Instead, we got to wait down here and stay out of Trouble with The Lord. That's how she says it, with capital letters, when she lets us out of the car at the church, "Stay out of Trouble with The Lord," she says and guns the engine so she can get her old Buick up the dirt road to the hilltop. The fattest aunt, she says she's got so many burdens to bear that the only solace she's got is to come up here to do the stations and remember the One Whose Burden Was Greatest. Sure don't look like she's getting any relief when she comes down from up there and we pile back into the cool blast of the air conditioning and see her thick face all shiny with sweat and strands of her hair sticking out from the bun she's always got on the back of her head. Looks more like suffering than relief, the way she's breathing heavy and got sweat stains circling her armpits.

We're supposed to stay right here, on the church steps, and not run over the graves in the cemetery, especially not the graves of our grandparents, the dead ones, that are buried right inside the gate. We can see the little round picture from here, stuck right in the center of their gravestone—somebody left open the little metal plate that's supposed to cover the picture. It's easy to see where the fattest aunt gets her fat from. Our grandpa, the dead one, is huge in that picture. He's round, and that's no exaggeration. Looks like he might not fit into the lens of just any old camera. Looks like that picture was taken with a very big camera.

We're also not supposed to wander off to the old white house over behind those trees, the one we can see the roof of from here, where the fattest aunt, our daddy, and all their brothers and sisters used to live with our grandparents, the dead ones. They lived there for a few years when our daddy was about our age, up until the owners kicked 'em all out 'cause they needed the house for their own kids or something. Our grandparents, the dead ones, took the fattest aunt, our daddy, and all the others and moved into a tent and a shack on another piece of land that our grandpa, the fat dead one, bought real cheap from his brother. We've been there—it's nothing but a rocky place with a few trees and the old shack on it.

There isn't anybody else around here, not even the pastor who lives in the rock house next to the church. His old Cadillac isn't in the carport, so he must have driven it into town or something. One of the windows on the front of the house looks like it's been broken by a rock. There's glass on the porch. We'll probably get blamed for it. Whenever anything turns up broken or missing, we're the ones that get our asses beat by the fattest aunt's husband. We don't even try to say we didn't do it anymore, 'cause he just says, "Well, even if you didn't do it this time, you thought about it, and you'll do it again some day. This is just to make sure you think twice about it next time," which doesn't make sense to us, but since he's the one with the big hands and wide belt, sense to us don't matter.

My sister likes to jump from the steps down to the ground. She's doing it now, starting from the first one and dropping down, then climbing to the second and jumping, then the third and so on. "I'm a parachuter jumping from a plane," she says as she leaps from the fourth step. "I'm James Bond escaping from the tall guy with bad teeth and a big belt," she says as she jumps from the fifth step. "I'm Indiana Jones," she starts to say as she jumps from the sixth step, but then she comes down wrong on her ankle and falls to the cement, scraping her knees up bad enough to bleed, and she starts crying.

From the road I hear some cars coming down the hill. "C'mon," I say to my sister. "It's the pest cars coming." They come by 'bout this time every few weeks when we're up here. Some car company uses these roads through the hills to test new kinds of cars. They come driving by, ten or fifteen at a time, a whining parade of flashy new white cars like the ones we never get to ride in. The fat grandpa, the dead one, used to call them pest cars 'cause they sound like some buzzing kind of bug as they swoosh past.

"One, two, three, four, five!" I count loudly as they whip by, and my sister yells with me, "Ten, 'leven, twelve, thirteen, fourteen, fifteen!" and then they're gone, swept with all their speed and noise round the hill.

We run back to the steps of the church to wait for the fattest aunt. After a while, we hear the wheels of her old Buick crunching on the gravel, coming down the hill like a big animal moving slow. She comes to a stop at the side of the church and me and my sister jump in, the cold air icing our heads while the fattest aunt says, "Hurry, *kindern,* close the door. This heat, it's a Trial, a real Trial," and we turn out onto the road to follow the pest cars into the city.

Remembering Falteen

1983 and 1985

Mostly I have to imagine Falteen—I did not know him. I met Falteen only twice—my great-uncle. We were at a wedding or a funeral, I don't remember which, when I met Uncle Falteen for the first time. It was at the church up to Honey Creek where my family either marries or buries, and I was only about ten years old. We went through whatever rituals were required, and the whole family went to the brick hall behind the church for the kinds of celebrations or consolations meals give to a family. My family eats largely—huge bubbling pots of beans, sweet rice, and meat—and their huge bellies reap the rewards of such grand appetites.

But Uncle Falteen looked more like a bird—some kind of hawk I would say now, though then I knew too little to know. He had an air about him that set him apart from my father's brothers and sisters, like he spent most of his time looking at things so small that nobody else could or would see them. He looked like he could lift from the ground if only he tried.

Not that he was slight exactly. That first time I saw Uncle Falteen leaves me with the strangely incompatible image of a strong-winged hawk rooted in the earth. His face was about as creased as any I've ever seen, a leather suitcase battered from its travels. One of my aunts led me over to where Uncle Falteen sat in the shade of a dusty pecan tree and introduced me.

"This is Nicklaus's boy," my aunt said, and Uncle Falteen looked into my eyes. "The one lives in Wisconsin."

Uncle Falteen looked at me in silence for a moment. He appeared old as stone, and everything seemed very exotic to me. I was a rootless boy wandering with my father wherever his truck driving jobs took him. These people, so many relatives gathered together and claiming one another for kin, made me feel like I'd walked into some tribal world.

"The oldest son of the oldest son." The way Uncle Falteen said it made it sound more like prophecy than a simple statement of fact. I was very still and watchful, waiting for something. Uncle Falteen's hawk eyes zeroed in on something that might have been me, or might have been somewhere behind me. "Some day that light in your eye gonna know where it needs to settle to shine" was the only other thing he said to me before one of my young cousins came bouncing across the hard, dry ground and jumped in Uncle Falteen's lap to be hugged and held. I retreated. Fear? Confusion? What did all this mean?

Later, when I was a few years older, my father took me along to the country place to set the sights of a new .22 he had bought for poaching deer. I sat in the cab of the truck between my father and Uncle Falteen, and I could smell their thick sweat and I wondered what mysterious process could convert the small smells of my own young body into the overpowering aroma of being a man.

They talked about things that I could only vaguely make sense of. Something secret seemed to dance around the edges of the words they spoke to one another without looking away from the cedar-scrubbed countryside unrolling around the truck. I closed my eyes and listened to my father and this stranger who kept calling him "nephew." Even though I'd met Falteen that once at Honey Creek, he still seemed mysterious to me.

When we arrived at the country place, they went immediately to work with the rifle. My father aimed toward a clump of cactus and said, "Upper right," while Uncle Falteen watched. When my father pulled the trigger, the quietness exploded, but the cactus did not move. "Wide right," Uncle Falteen said, and my father adjusted the sights. The next shot nicked the upper right corner of the cactus pad. "Should a been a dead center hit," my father said and set to work again, tinkering with the sight's fine tuning. On the next shot, he was satisfied with the setting, and they began testing one another, stepping off thirty paces from a thick cluster of cactus, and alternating shots. Then stepping off another ten paces, and going through the gun trade again.

By that time my head was throbbing from the explosive noises, and the smell of gunfire hung thick in my nose, coated my tongue. I wandered off to the shack where my father had lived as a child. It was in rough shape, holes showing through the planks and tarpaper ripped around the edges. I pushed open the door that my father said he'd built himself. It was a heavy door, cobbled together out of scavenged boards and nails. It still fit snug in the doorframe, the only part of the run-down building that still functioned properly.

Inside, the light was dim, and the sound of the rifle muffled by the walls was less insistent. I sat down on the rusted seat of a metal folding chair and lay my head on my forearms as they rested on a rough wooden table. I tried to think about what I would tell my sister about this trip to the country place, but no words came. I sat there feeling the pressure of my cheek against my forearm. I felt sick.

After a few minutes I raised my head and looked around the room. My eyes had adjusted to the dim light, and I noticed things I hadn't seen before. There were a number of dusty glass jars along the table in front of me, and they were full of powdery white stuff that might be flour or insect poisons. The metal lids of the jars were rusty in places. One had rusted all the way through, and the powdery stuff inside had gotten wet, then dried to a caked hardness, and I thought of my father's current job. Every night he came home from the lime plant covered with white soot.

There was a canvas tacked to one wall. It was one of Opa Ben's paintings—a young boy tossing a ball into the air with a dog leaping beside him, tongue hanging out. My father had one of Opa Ben's paintings hanging in the living room—a buck with head half turned to look back into the snowy forest behind him. But this painting on the wall of the shack was the first I'd seen where my grandfather had painted a human figure.

The boy was huge, his bones massive and loaded with flesh. I looked down at my own skinny body and remembered my mother's joke about me being the milkman's son. My father, my grandfather, my uncles and aunts, even this imagined boy in the painting all had big bones and solid muscles. The imaginary boy in the painting seemed to have more claim to being part of this family than I did.

The boy in the painting did not look like he was enjoying himself with that ball he was tossing. His big head tilted back to look at the red-and-white striped ball, and a small straw sombrero hung from a string behind his back. The boy's mouth was set, a look of resignation, as if he expected that ball to just keep going up into the sky, never to be seen again. The dog's silly grin added to this impression. The boy was losing, yet again, something he had allowed himself to love a little.

While I was looking at that painting, small-boned Uncle Falteen walked into the open square of the doorway.

"Let's go on down to get a drink of McCurdy Creek water," he had said. "Best thing I know for a damned headache."

I had been surprised that Uncle Falteen knew I felt sick. My father never paid attention to what kinds of things I felt or liked. Once, when my father was driving over-the-road, I rode along with him for a few weeks, and my father ordered cheeseburgers and chocolate milk for me at every stop, morning, noon, or night. I hated cheeseburgers. I grew to hate chocolate milk too. I'd neither drunk chocolate milk nor eaten hamburgers since, but my father never noticed, and still sometimes called me by the CB handle he gave me—"Cheeseburger and Chocolate Milk."

"Come on," Uncle Falteen said. "We can walk down, and your pa can pick us up there when he's finished killing cactus."

We went out together through a drooping gate, and Uncle Falteen led the way down the road. We walked slow, and Uncle Falteen pointed at the way the split-tailed birds flew level for a short distance, then went into a perpendicular climb and then made a breakneck plummeting dive, tittering crazily all the time.

"They're telling us its gonna storm," Uncle Falteen said without breaking stride. "Oma Scheel used to call them stormbirds, 'cause they always acted like that before it rained."

I nodded, although I had no idea whether my uncle was telling a story like the ones my father sometimes told. I had a sense, however, that if it *was* a story, it was a good one, meant not to harm, but to get me to pay attention to the things going on around me, take my mind off myself.

We came over a slight rise in the road and looked down on the low-water crossing of the creek. The water glimmered over the road in the late afternoon light, and I told Uncle Falteen the creek looked like silver.

"No, not silver. Gold," Uncle Falteen had said. "See that house over there," he pointed to a rambling rock building tucked under a stand of old live oaks and looking down a gentle slope to the creek. "That's Old Nick Gulden's place. He was such a rich guy that the water here runs gold, like his name. Nephew," he squeezed my shoulder gently, firmly. The pressure of touch seemed like a gift. "You are about to discover the absolute medicinal value of gold creek water for healing headaches, heartburn, and all around mopishness."

As we walked down to the water, I felt light, like I might begin to float—like I could keep right on walking across the creek, and not even get my shoes wet. We squatted in the road and drank from the stream right where it ran over the eroded concrete of the crossing. The water, cold on my tongue, tasted sharp and clean. I drank from cupped palms and splashed my face, and the taste of gunpowder was washed from my tongue. My headache disappeared.

Uncle Falteen startled me with a deep-throated chuckle and then a full, guffawing laugh.

"That's some cushion you found to sit on," Falteen said and pointed.

I was sitting in freshly laid cow dung. The manure clung when I tried to brush it from my pants, but I found myself laughing too. It didn't matter much while I sat there listening to my great-uncle's laughter and feeling the sun on my face. Even years later, those few minutes sitting beside the river, trying to wipe the stain on the short grass and listening to my great-uncle tell how he used to work laying up hay for Old Man Gulden seem about as crystalline and pure as the taste of that spring-fed creek. When my dad rattled down the hill in the truck, I climbed up, manure-stained pants and all, and lay alone in the bed of the pickup. All the way back down to San Antonio I watched the way the sky seemed so big that it swallowed the clouds. I had never before felt so entirely inside myself.

The Graveyard under the Hill

1992

Family stories—a ground, an earth for me to walk on. It is the kind of place to walk that Susan Wood describes in her poem, "Campo Santo."

> . . . *Campo santo,* they call it,
> *holy field,* and even those without belief
> say it is blessed by the dead who lie there,
> because, surely, all of them were loved once
> by someone. Some of them are still remembered.

My family's stories, my own stories, my own family stories.

After an Easter morning service I ride with my aunts and uncles and cousins to the cemetery at Honey Creek where Opa Ben and Oma Aurelia are buried. After a collective prayer of thanksgiving for these tired and harsh people who were our parents and grandparents, we walk around the cemetery at the base of the hill and look at other gravestones.

Aunt Virginia and Uncle Stephen try to explain to me how each of the people buried here is related to me. In a storytelling sense, this re-membering of family invites me into a group of kin in which these buried people are in the present as much as any of my cousins rolling around in the grass and the warm sunshine of the cemetery.

One woman, Great-aunt Lucia, is re-membered only for how she died. Uncle Stephen says, "And that's Mathilda Kuntz. She's your great-grand-cousin, once removed, on Mama's side. She got bit by a rattler in, I think, 1915 or something," and he bends close to look at the grave marker, a rusted wrought-iron cross. "No, it was in 1916. She was out toward the creek to get water, and she got bit by a snake. She didn't have nobody with her, so she had to go on walking home." Aunt Virginia interrupts: "She ran. That girl ran and ran, which, you know, you just can't do." I say, "It makes the blood circulate faster. . . ." And Aunt Virginia: "So the poison goes right to the heart." Uncle Stephen finishes, "So she died long time before any of us were born."

Straining my eyes in the sunlight, reading a name I've never known before, I'm amazed at the way the three of us have just re-created Mathilda, made her again a member of our family's story, as if we had all been there on that serpent-filled morning, as if we're describing events that have just now happened.

By the time we reach the end of the graveyard, I am beginning to wonder what kinds of changes have taken place in my thinking and in my emotions—the results of my re-entry into the life of this family and this place, Honey Creek. My cousins run off to get a drink of water at the fountain down by the church, and the adults sit down in the shadow of a live oak to rest for a few minutes before starting the drive back to the city.

I walk out through the cemetery gate, and climb toward the top of the hill where the path with the stations of the cross marks time and place. I'm going to see what there is to see.

The courtyard of a Fredericksburg restaurant and beer garden. Photograph taken in early 1970s, just before the town's economy accelerated into a tourism boom.

Part 3

Migrations toward Home

FREDERICKSBURG, TEXAS

Whilst writing I often keep thinking of home. It is usually assumed that a sense of place or belonging gives a person stability. But what makes a place a home? Is it wherever your family is, where you have been brought up? The children of many migrants are not sure where they belong. Where is home? Is it where your parents are buried? Is home the place from where you have been displaced, or where you are now? Is home where your mother lives? And, then, we speak of "home away from home". I am moved when I am asked the phenomenological question "Are you at home in the world?" In certain places and at certain times, I am. I feel secure and friendly to others. But at other times I feel that I don't know where I am.

Madan Sarup, "Home and Identity," in *Travellers' Tales: Narratives of Home and Displacement*

Climbing under Fences, Looking for Stories

Legends of the most varied sort are found in the predominantly German community of Fredericksburg. Most common are the several tales connected with the Fredericksburg Easter Fires, but tales of practically every category are found in this Prusso-American Community.

William J. Campion, *The Lore and Legend of the Texas Hill Country*

Hill country town at night: Hands, arms, worn blue oilcloth—they were partially visible in the yellow square of a kitchen window as I walked by in the street. Vines grew around the window, framing it. A dog was barking in the yard. Someone coughed on the dark front porch. I walked on. It was just a little past nine o'clock. The town was quiet, adjusting to summertime dark. On another block another house: huge, silent, looming, empty. Crickets made peaceful sounds from the picket fence weeds; there was a high singing from tree frogs in the hackberry trees. Down the street a boy was slanting through a vacant lot. He fired his BB gun twice into the shadows, waited for a moment, fired once more, then disappeared. A porch light burned at a corner house. Beneath the light a pair of old man's shoes sat in a wooden swing. I walked, finally, to the edge of town, where the narrow, unpaved street turned off into country darkness. In a grassy lot a long wooden building waited behind its faded sign for travelers who seldom came anymore.

Elroy Bode, *This Favored Place: The Texas Hill Country*

For three days I've thought about doing this: riding my bike long after dark out to Cross Mountain at the edge of town, my squeaky chain waking the air with the howls of distant unseen dogs, the waning half-moon faint and yellow as it comes up in the east. When I was in high school I used to walk in my neighborhood late at night, and sometimes, without seeking to pry, I would see into the lit windows of houses and glimpse storied fragments of those people's lives. Tonight, as someone writing about this place, I am still doing this: looking into other people's backlit windows, hoping to catch fragments of the stories of their lives.

At the mountain, I climb through the narrow opening set up like a

maze to prevent cattle from entering. I go slowly along the road winding round to the top. In daylight I never go this way. I crawl under a
washout in the fence and take one of many shortcuts up the sides, but
in the darkness I don't know my way here, and though it is too cool for
rattlesnakes to be active, the darkness might conceal a nearby skunk or
cactus. So I stick to the cleared road.

I might be breaking some curfew. The mountain's grounds might be
off limits after dark. Perhaps a policeman will find me here, and force
me to explain my night shadowy presence in the hills. Below the mountain I hear a gaggle of domestic geese squabble briefly, then fall silent.

Atop the hill, I sit for a moment on the stone set in the ground beneath the cross and look out at the town lights spreading across the valley, trickling up the surrounding slopes. The stone I'm sitting on has a
memorial on it: "In memory of Christian Durst who found the original
cross on this hill in 1847." And in smaller print: "Donated by Roland
Kaderli." On the Saturday night before Easter Sunday, they still light a
bonfire here allegedly to commemorate the return of a founding father,
John Meusebach, from a meeting with the Comanche Indians. They say
Meusebach concluded a treaty with the Comanche that enabled the
Germans to settle this area in relative peace. Francis Edward Abernathy
describes this event in "Texas Folklore and German Culture" (in Wilson 1977, 85–86).

The legend around here is that Christian, who arrived in the area
with the first German settlers to come this far into the Hill Country,
found an old wooden cross atop this mountain. Nobody seems to know
who raised those first timbers, but writers who retell the legend suggest it was either a Spanish missionary or one of his Native American
converts.

There's a painting hanging in the town library of the mountain with
that first cross atop it, but the cross itself has been successively replaced
with other wooden ones until 1979, when the historical society erected a
metal cross set into a concrete base. They installed lights later in order
to make this reminder of faith—whether the anonymous Spaniard's, the
equally unknown Native American's, Christian's, Roland's, or the collective faith of the community—visible at night as well as during the
day. This late, however, the lights are off, and I sit with only dark metal
and concrete behind me.

Except for the dense lights along Main Street, and the cluster around the hospital, I imagine I could easily count every streetlight in the valley, and from this distance they look as much like campfires as streetlights. But in reality, there are too many to easily number, so I stand and slowly turn in a full circle to count the pulsating lights of seventeen radio and television towers beyond the rim of the valley.

The steady stream of trucks that usually rumbles through town on Main Street has slowed with the early morning hour. I'm told truckers call Fredericksburg "Stop-and-Go-ville" because Main Street also serves as U.S. Highway 290, and the dozen stoplights never seem to be timed right to make it through without stopping for at least half of them.

The first time I came to Fredericksburg a few years ago, I stayed because Fredericksburg felt like a place where the past is remembered and used as a basis for sustaining everyday life in ways unremembered in urban places like Houston and Dallas. Before I drove the eighty miles from Austin, where I was visiting my sister, to Fredericksburg, I wrote in my journal: "I had this idea that I would teach myself how to live in cities using San Antonio as my test field. Why do I need to live in cities? There *are* still villages. That is where I am going." That entry was equal parts defiance, petulance, and frustration. I hadn't been able to get my bearings straight in San Antonio, and the city scattered my attempts to find a place to live and a job to support myself there.

So I came to Fredericksburg seeking a small town with the feeling of a "village," and, of course, I found it. Standing atop Cross Mountain now, looking down at these could-be-campfires, I still see this is such a *heimlich*, homelike, place. Even if it is a deliberately promoted and preserved *heimlichkeit*, homelikeness.

But the flashing lights of those radio and television towers that surround the valley, the new buildings going up on Main Street to house "Wild West" shops, and the way I've had to take tourism-dependent jobs warn me not to romanticize this town away from its place in the contemporary world. They remind me that the pull to this place and my response to it have not been simple.

I've been moving most of my life, and it's not so much because I've wanted to, but it seems that's just the way it always has been. Sometimes I'd like nothing better than to settle down in some little house with a garden and get on with the real work of tending a place. I've come close a few times, but to this day, every time I start getting established someplace, something comes up and I've got to move on. I suppose my upbringing has something to do with it. My father had less economic savvy even than I, and consequently feet even more restless than mine; we moved every couple of years so he could get away from his creditors and "start all over" again. And again. And yet again. We spent so much of my growing up time starting over and over that it's a wonder I know how to finish anything at all. Maybe I don't.

I thought that might be an important thing to say, since I'm telling a story about a place where I have lived only intermittently.

The first time I came to town, I loved the initial feeling of welcome I received, but that first welcome became opaque as I tried to make lasting connections with people, connections that would go deeper than simple pleasantries while standing in line at the store or the bank. Feeling like I was living only the sketchy outline of a life, I had to leave in search of some place more sustaining to who I was then.

Now I've returned to this place, to try once again to climb under the fence to hear the stories of the place. It takes time, and a certain kind of bored patience, this opening into the stories of a community, especially a community that so successfully obscures its private lights in the darkness of telling and retelling its public history and myths in books and everyday conversation.

The Storyteller's Dead

Liking Enchanted Rock is probably a matter of temperament. Some visitors find it bare and boring, worth a ten-minute stay on its top and no more. To others it is a melancholy, clear echo of the Texas of Indian times. They like its simplicity, the spaciousness of the world around it, and the persistence with which life clings to it—a few plants and animals keeping stubbornly alive on what seems to be nothing but hard granite.

Richard Phelan, *Texas Wild: The Life, Plants, and Animals of the Lone Star State*

As the beauty of many a desert flower is spent without ever a human eye to delight in it, so the rich talents of at least one of Gillespie County's first settlers were totally wasted. That settler was Peter Berg, who in later years has been called "Hermit of the Hills." At the age of twenty years Berg came to America from Germany, on the ship *Iris,* landing at Indianola, Texas, in January, 1857, after an eight weeks voyage. . . . His betrothed had remained in Germany. Berg planned to earn money in America and then provide passage for her to join him. This he did, plying his fickle trade as an excellent stone mason. But his fair lady had faint and fickle heart; it seems that tales about the frontier made her decide not to go there but to marry another and stay near the coast. Peter Berg, in deep disappointment, withdrew from society. About eight miles east of Fredericksburg, on land to which he had no legal claim, he built a hermitage. For it he used the natural walls of a ravine and filled in the rest with masonry.

Gillespie County Historical Society, *Pioneers in God's Hills*

I drive along Ranch Road 935 to Enchanted Rock, and spend the day climbing around on the smaller granite formation called the Little Dome, which sits beside the bald curve of the Rock itself. I prefer the smaller mountain because it is less monolithic, less opaquely whole than the larger Rock. There are more cracks in the Little Dome, and more small canyons that you can climb into and watch the play of light and shadows on the rough granite surface of the rocks. When you finally come out on the top of the smaller dome, you find quite a few vernal pools, places where water collects in the spring and offers a chance for vegetation to take hold. Some of the plants in these isolated pools grow nowhere else in the world. They are isolated here because they can only grow where granite offers the proper minerals. The geological formation known as the Llano Uplift sits at the center of Texas, a pink granite heart surrounded on all sides by bony limestone. The plants remain concentrated in their indigenous place.

I climb over and down the smaller dome, and find a place where dozens of buzzards—turkey vultures—roost on the side of the larger Rock. Beneath their roosting place is a sheer granite wall that makes a strong echo, so I sit down to play my flute and listen to the rock throw the music back to me. The buzzards remain unperturbed on their perches.

Near sunset, clouds close in, and I hurry back to my truck to avoid slipping on the rock. When granite is dry, it provides ideal footing—thus Enchanted Rock's reputation as the best rock-climbing spot in the state—but when the surface gets wet, not even the best climber, which I am far from being, can maintain a footgrip. I sit in the cab of the pickup for a while and watch the rain douse the Rock and slick down the sides. It looks like the egg of a giant buzzard exposed to a sudden storm without the parent bird's clutching feathers to protect it.

I drive back along 935 for a few miles until I see a sign pointing the way to Lower Crabapple Road. I know this road runs into the backside of Fredericksburg somewhere, so I turn onto it, and drive slowly over cattleguards and around several drenched cows that refuse to move their wet bodies. The road follows along Crabapple Creek, and in the dimming light, I can see a ridge of hills high enough to be called mountains around here.

By the time I reach Fredericksburg, it has grown dark, and I don't know exactly what part of town I've driven into. I make a wrong turn, and find myself pointed north again, toward Llano, and when I turn around and drive back toward the town center, I unexpectedly pass a bar where I used to drink a few beers when I lived in Fredericksburg before. The bartender (who was also the owner) had been the first stranger to ever buy me a beer.

When I walk in, I see that the bartender is not the same woman, but someone much younger.

"Does Zita still own this place?" I ask.

"Oh, yeah," the woman answers. "She and Wayne are at home tonight. What can I get you?"

I order a beer.

"And where have you been?" says a thirtyish-looking man sitting on a barstool while I wait for her to bring my drink.

"Uh . . . I've been at Enchanted Rock all day," I manage to say, though I'm a bit intimidated by the man's demanding tone.

"And?" He doesn't seem satisfied.

"And . . . um . . . I walked around all afternoon."

"And?" But this time I have nothing more to answer. Am I being called down for looking like an outsider with my long hair and goatee-beard? I stand there trying to recall the last time I got into a fight, and have to go all the way back to sixth grade for a relevant memory.

"And," the man says with a broad grin when the bartender brings my beer, "You're thirsty!"

I suppose my relief is visible as I sit down on a barstool a few places away from his.

"I want to introduce you to one of the finest Texans in the world," he says to me and turns to the man beside him, who is slightly younger. "This is Mike."

We reach across the stools and shake hands. "And what about this other fine Texan?" I ask, nodding to the man who has mock-confronted me.

"He's Bobby," Mike says.

"My name is Bobby," says my imagined brawler. "Are you from around here?"

I explain that my father's family comes from a bit further south, and when Bobby asks what I do for a living, I explain my research to him. Then I ask him the same two questions.

"I'm born and raised in Gillespie. I could tell you about any place in the county," he answers, and then his face grows solemn. "I'm a mortician."

I can't think of an intelligent thing to say, so I remain silent while Mike snickers a little.

"You laugh," Bobby says as he turns to his friend, "but it's not funny."

"It's an important job," I say, trying to be helpful. "Taking care of the dead's important."

Bobby nods.

"You'd be easy to take care of," he says. "Skinny guy like you, wouldn't take much. It's the fat ones that give you trouble."

Mike laughs again, and after Bobby glares at him, he gets up and beats a retreat to the bathroom.

"How long have you been doing this?" I ask.

"I've been a mortician for six years now."

"Is there anything like a burnout point? Do you see a time when it will just become too much?"

"Well, doing family is easy," he says. "You *know* family. You've seen them, and you know what they've done, what their life has been like. Although it might be hard if I ever have to do one of my own kids."

I'm nodding understandingly, listening like a tape recorder.

"But friends, now friends are a different thing," he says as Mike returns. "Working on friends is hard."

"Bobby Burg," Mike says, swallowing an out-and-out guffaw. "You are something!"

"Your last name is Berg?" I ask. I'm remembering the story of Peter

Berg, a hermit around here during the nineteenth century. I read the story while I was living in Fredericksburg a few years ago. He built himself a pipe organ out of old newspapers, and a stone tower from which to watch the stars and predict the weather. I romanticized him as a model of isolated creativity during that first period in town, which was something of a hermitage for me as well.

"Do you know anything about this guy, his name was Berg too, who lived around here in the last century?" I ask. "He was supposed to have a hermitage outside town. I'd love to see that place."

"You mean Peter Berg?" Bobby says. "Oh yeah, I even know where he's buried. Him and his wife."

"I don't think this guy was married," I protest. "He was suppose to have been a hermit."

"Oh, well, he was married," Bobby says. "You can see his grave out there by the Grape Creek School. It says 'P-e-t-e-r B-u-r-g *Gestorben* —that's German for died—March 9, 1864. And above that it says Mathilda, *Gestorben* March 5, 1864."

"We must be talking about different people," I say. "I think this hermit died later than that, and his name was spelled 'B-*e*-r-g,' which is German for 'mountain.'"

"Well, the story is that some of my kinfolk got into a fight years ago," Bobby says. "Some of them moved over there to where Burg's Corner is now. They moved away and changed the spelling of their name to distinguish themselves from the other Bergs."

Our conversation turns briefly to other topics, including the length of my hair and our astrological signs. I note to myself the oddness of sitting in a bar in a small Texas town and discussing the relative merits of different character signs with a native mortician. Bobby tells me he is a Leo, and Mike, who is from New Braunfels, and who knows some of the same people I've heard my uncle talk about, is a Taurus.

"My father's a Leo too," I tell Bobby.

Our conversation is interrupted by someone who has come in and recognizes Bobby. They haven't seen one another in several years, so they talk to catch up. This person asks Bobby,

"You still working for that roofing outfit?"

"No," Bobby says. "I haven't worked for them for a long time. I'm not working. Taking unemployment right now."

I assume he doesn't want to break the mood of good feeling with his mortician conversation-stopper, but after the man goes back to the friends he's walked in with, Bobby turns to me and says, "I can't lie to you anymore. I'm not a mortician, I'm telling you a story. Leos are storytellers."

Mike bursts out laughing as I say, "You are a storyteller just like my father!"

Coda, Two Days Later: On my way to Austin, I stop at Grape Creek School to check out whether Bobby's other story—the one about a Peter Burg being buried there—was equally fabricated. I take a picture of the combined headstone of Peter and Mathilda. I'll give it to Bobby as a memorial to the dead he never worked on the next time I see him.

Public Stories/Private Pasts

Hill Country Germans are both beneficiaries and the victims of this new turn of events. Their towns are awash in new wealth, new jobs have proliferated, old buildings are being preserved, and their history is being "honored." But the honoring is curiously defined in ways that often seem quite inappropriate and oddly misplaced. Public life emerges as a kind of entertainment ritual, with bands, balloons, costumes, and flags, but with little context or substance. The view of the past, while commercially entertaining, has little connection with what actually happened. What is at work here is the trivialization of public memory and public life. In the process, a society runs the risk of losing the sense of its own history as a commonweal, and eventually a sense of its own values.

Lawrence Goodwyn, *Coming to Terms:*
The German Hill Country of Texas

A long time ago a man in Fredericksburg sold his skin to the devil. This bargain was made so that the man could have unlimited material wealth and pleasure. The agreement was satisfactory to both parties for a short time, but soon the man began to think that he had made a bad deal. As he thought about it, he decided to break the agreement. The youth ran through town yelling to the devil and saying he wanted his skin back. Satan was aggravated, but he finally tossed the man's skin back to him.

William J. Campion, *The Lore and Legend of the Texas Hill Country*

Nostalgia pervades this town and these hills. A rough estimate might place the number of antique shops in the Hill Country in the hundreds. In the town of Fredericksburg alone, places selling memorabilia, souvenirs, reminders and trinkets connected to the history of the German settlers of Texas well exceeds thirty. I could walk the three-mile strip of the main street and not go more than a few steps at a time without some visual or verbal reminder that this is a place of "history." Preserved limestone buildings: The White Elephant Saloon (now a weaving studio); The Old Domino Hall Antiques; Das Peachhouse Restaurant; Das Peach Haus Gifts; Sunday House Smoked Meats. Sometimes, in my less complacent moments, I find myself thinking that Fredericksburg has sold its skin to the devil of heritage tourism.

There was a time only about sixty years ago when the Fredericksburg Chamber of Commerce felt it necessary to extol the virtues of the town's many "modern" conveniences: "Keidel Memorial Hospital, one of the city's fine medical institutions, modernly equipped, completely staffed"; "Gillespie County's modern courthouse, erected in 1939"; "St. Mary's Parochial School, a modern institution of learning." These are all photo captions from the guidebook *Fredericksburg: In the Texas Hill Country*, published in the mid-1940s.

Today the guidebooks take the opposite approach: "Fredericksburg is one of the most picturesque small towns in Texas and conscious of it," says a recent *Eyes of Texas Travel Guide*. Now we are reminded that the stone structures that stand restored on almost every city street were handbuilt by pioneers, and are testaments to the historical tenacity and solidity of these German settlers. Parades and festivals display Germanness publicly, and during Oktoberfest, for a price everybody gets a chance to drink German beer and dance a polka to music performed by an odd assortment of bands. At my first Oktoberfest, where I worked as a janitor, I heard a band that consisted of a German woman and her husband from India wearing a cowboy hat and playing polkas on his electric piano.

What room does this public display of *Deutschlichkeit* leave for the private realities of contemporary Hill Country residents? In fact, does a space for memory exist in the midst of such a profusion of public commemoration? The German Hill Country is suffused with heritage tourism, but where is the history and the memory of the people who live here?

A brief story from my first period living in the Hill Country suggests the difficulty in answering these questions: I talked to a successful furniture store owner whose family had been in Fredericksburg since its founding in the mid-1840s. We sat on the sales floor in two of his recliners and talked about his family history. His stories, however, were equal parts personal memory and recitation from history books. He told me a funny personal story about working in a 1930s "curb service" pharmacy, and then he told me a story about the loss of early county records in a courthouse fire. The second story was recited almost verbatim from a local history book I had been reading prior to our talk. He told both stories with the same "I was there" narrative voice.

My intention is to explore the above questions by weaving together "historical" sources, ethnographic observation, and my own family's creation of storytelling opportunities. I am seeking to observe the blockages and opportunities for collective re-memorying that Hill Country residents create. I want to understand how people speak of and for themselves in the interstices of a public display and consumption of history aimed at attracting tourist income to an area that might otherwise be economically underdeveloped in the contemporary world.

History in the Hills

The facts of history are a fleeting succession of images flashed onto the mind. That successive generations interpret and arrange and weigh these images differently, in light of their different experiences, loads the past with a fruitful variety of dynamic meanings.

The past is never finished, never final. It lives on, changing from generation to generation. Each new generation must rewrite its own history to explain an ever-changing present. Each generation looks to discover in its past the combinations to unlock the possibilities of its future.

In a larger sense, then, history is a progression of metaphors, never static, but constantly changing as the light strikes them differently. These metaphors illuminate the present and reflect the future. They grow from our need to believe, to create myths and heroes, to chalk our way into a better tomorrow.

This was the ethical dream of many nineteenth-century German colonists in Texas: to rearrange the pieces of their past so that they would have a new future—in short, to make a new world. In a very active way, they took history into their own hands.

> Glen E. Lich, "Introduction," in *German Culture in Texas:*
> *A Free Earth*

I am standing atop a low hill of history. Beneath me I might look at history as a winding time line stretched out across the landscape of the past like a creek. This stream unfolds through time and at one end I see Carl, Prince of Solms-Braunfels, as he writes words praising the benefits of looking inward and back to the German homeland as a way to maintain old-world customs and manners:

> There are in Texas, thanks be to the Lord, those among the older settlers who have not yet forgotten their country and its good and pious customs and live in accordance with them . . . Fortunate are those Germans who, in spite of their colonization among such people whose language they do not understand and whose habits remain strange, are able to establish new homes which will differ little from those of their fatherland. They associate with their own countrymen, hear nothing but German spoken, and, albeit on this side of the ocean, find also the customs of their native country.

> (Carl, Prince of Solms-Braunfels, *Texas 1844–1846*)

Prince Carl stands over by the spring. In 1846 he's at the beginning of the European settlement of these hills, negotiating for a piece of property that he has never seen. But he knows, or at least he writes, that the key to maintaining cultural identity will be the isolation of the German immigrants who arrive in Texas under the sponsorship of a society of German noblemen, an *Adelsverein*. Established in 1842, this society of German nobles promised to provide free land-claims and economic support for German colonists to Texas. With an organizational structure somewhere between a corporation (colonists paid for "shares" in the venture) and a philanthropic "nobles network," the venture failed rather spectacularly, resulting in many deaths and difficulties for the thousands (estimates range from 6,000 to 10,000) of Germans who eventually traveled to Texas under the *Adelsverein*'s ostensible support. Otto W. Tetzlaff concisely described this group in "A Guide for German Immigrants" (in Wilson 1977).

Downstream in 1968—in an idyllic little meadow beside the creek—stands Joe B. Frantz creating a nostalgic present by praising the wonderful abilities of the Anglos, the Germans, and the Mexicans of the Hill Country to both mix and maintain their distinct cultural heritages:

> Primarily they came from Anglo-Saxon, German, and Mexican stock. The most frequent names are names like Johnson, Weinheimer, or Flores. They do an adroit and effective job both of mingling and of maintaining their separate identities. A Saturday night German dance behind Fischer's General Store is a latter twentieth-century version of an old-time frontier cabin raising, except that beer replaces the rum. . . . It is community fun at its liveliest, and no one cares whether you speak with a straight Texas twang, pronounce your "f's" as if they were "pf's," or call out Julio as if it were spelled "Hulio." The idea is that you are all God's creatures, from babes who can barely amble to octogenarians who can't walk much firmer. (J. R. White 1968)

These are two points in time, historical bookends of sorts. And I am here, on the hill of the present, able to see the circle that includes Prince Carl in 1846, and Joe B. in 1968. I am in a position to notice things about each of these men's words that neither had the chance to observe. Prince Carl, an aristocrat faced with what he considers rough and rude manners on a frontier, argues for isolation; Joe B., living at a time when multicultural awareness first gained legitimacy, sees racial harmony in diversity.

Here I stand in the Hill Country of my own time, and notice that both men were describing a place they imagined and, to some extent, made possible with their imaginings. The Germans of the Hill Country did manage to maintain their own cultural world for a hundred years or more by following a strategy very much like Carl's isolationist plan, but they could not entirely ignore the Anglos, Mexicans, and others around them. In fact, the early German settlers absolutely depended on the intervention of a nearby colony of Mormons to teach them how to farm the thin-soiled and rain-scarce region. Local historians and guidebooks often retell the story of the intervention of nearby Mormons who saved the German settlers from starvation in the early years of settlement. A regional Hill Country culture that weaves together German, Mexican, and Anglo influences has developed.

The image I see from my historical hill, however, is a bit less harmonious than Joe B.'s ahistoricized snapshot. In 1990, during my first sojourn in the Hill Country, I applied for a job at a turkey processing plant in Fredericksburg. Sitting in the office of the plant's manager—an Anglo man engaged to a German descendant in the area—I was informed that I "didn't want to work on the processing line" (the job I had seen advertised in the paper). I was reminded that as a capable young man I "wanted something more visible, with room for advancement. Maybe a job driving a yard truck." I was told that moving live turkeys around in cages was preferable to opening the bodies of dead turkeys and pulling out their internal organs. Then I heard a contemporary version of the relationship between various ethnic groups in the Hill Country: "Most big turkey plants have machines to do the eviscerating and cleaning. In this plant, our machines is a Mexican with a knife."

I took no job there—neither on the processing line nor in the yard truck—but I learned an important lesson about the public appearances and private practices of the area to which I had returned. Despite the harmonious assessment of Joe B. Frantz, this has been, and remains, an area with racial tensions, sometimes submerged in air-conditioned offices, sometimes exposed to the dazzling heat of the Hill Country sun. The stories within my own family suggest that this has been the case historically as well, as suggested by the story in Part 2 about the Mexican man looking for lunch and being chased away by my grandfather's shotgun.

"My father, of course, was prejudiced," Uncle Herbert said after telling me that story. "My father wouldn't have shot him—there probably weren't even any shells in that gun, but he knew it would scare him. He didn't want Mexicans around with all those kids. He didn't want them around at all; he was very prejudiced. And it's sort of inbred in us too. We're not overly welcoming sometimes."

Founder's Day

1. Henry Kammlah

They are great home lovers, and with them their own blood kin comes first and last. They provide for their families and plan for their descendants. This accounts for the fact that it is no uncommon thing to find even the third or fourth generation of Germans living in the same farming community, and sons succeeding fathers in mercantile and banking concerns.

Don H. Biggers, 1925, placard in Fredericksburg Pioneer Museum

Yet for all its strength and wisdom, the rural environment does not seem to be weathering well. More and more rural Texans, sitting on family holdings worth in many instances far more than the villas of their oil-rich city cousins, find that they can hardly support themselves and pay taxes from the income that their land produces. The emerging rural scene shows increasing disparity of wealth. The "land wealthy" have not been able to keep their homesteads up.

Glen E. Lich, "The Rural Scene in Texas," in *Texas Country: The Changing Rural Scene*

Every year since 1981, the Fredericksburg Historical Society has celebrated the descendants of pioneers with its Founder's Day in early May. In 1993, I wandered in and between the structures that were built by pioneers, then rebuilt by the people—descendants and newcomers alike—who have, in time, replaced those pioneers. Henry Kammlah was born in the building that now houses the Pioneer Museum owned by the Society.

I met him while I sat under the breezy tent at the entrance to the museum grounds with Edmund and Rosalie Kaseri. Edmund is a "native-born" resident who lived elsewhere for fifty years and moved back into town six years ago. Rosalie said to me, "It's the retirees that support this town. They're the ones who pay the taxes. Them and the few old-timers who are large landowners. They'll have a place in town and a place in the country."

When Henry Kammlah walked up, Mr. Kaseri introduced us and we talked for some time while people passed in and out of the grounds through a wooden gate set into the fence. Some people stopped to greet

Henry and Edmund by name, others shyly looked away from the small group of "locals" talking under the tent. I wondered whether they could tell that I am as new to this place as many of them.

"I remember when I was a little boy," Henry said. "I went out into the middle of the street out there, and when I looked up the road I saw a damned herd of cattle come running this way, so I went in and told my father and he come out and closed that gate in a hurry," Henry said, pointing to where the crowd passed through the opening in the fence.

"I guess that explains one of the reasons those stone walls are there." I pointed to the high wall around the churchyard across the street.

"They weren't building those things just for decoration," Henry affirmed.

"What's it like to see all these people wandering around the place where you grew up?"

"I'll tell you, I'm glad my sisters sold this place to the museum. You don't know what damned thing would have happened to it otherwise."

"When did you move out of this house?"

"I went into the service in '42, and my sisters inherited that house when I got the ranch."

"Do you live in town now, or in the country?"

"I live right out here on the edge of town." He points north. "I did that work [on the ranch] for sixty years, but I can't do it no more account of my damned knees. I got a good man to lease it, but it just doesn't seem right."

"Don't you have any children who could do it?"

"I've got a boy in San Antonio, a girl in Brenham, and another boy in the service. I thought one of them might take over the place, but none of them ever did. It just doesn't seem right."

Henry's wife walked up to the tent, and after a brief introduction, she and Henry left to go home.

"Come by Andy's cafe sometime," he said. "We all sit there and tell bear stories to one another."

2. Sarah Austin

As people search for reconnections on the Edwards Plateau, there is something in the German frontier struggle that does shine through. The Germans of the Texas Hill Country created a mode of living that was a powerful expression of nineteenth-century American striving.

Self-reliance was more than an attribute of self; it was part of society's belief in the value of work and the interrelatedness of individual effort to the collective vitality of the community. This blend of individual self-respect and collective self-confidence—this vision of the citizen commonwealth—gave shape to the past and meaning to daily life. It is this vision that is obscured in commercialized civic ritual.

Lawrence Goodwyn, *Coming to Terms: The German Hill Country of Texas*

Using dyes from plants is an ancient craft, rich in history and tradition. Of course, it's outdated today by modern industry and chemical technology. Everybody knows you can buy colored yarn and don't have to make it yourself. But to a dyer, that's beside the point. Dyeing is fun, it's full of surprises, it's a little like magic.

Rita Buchanan, *A Weaver's Garden*

The museum buildings include the old Kammlah house and barn, a *fachwork* cabin transported to the grounds from elsewhere and restored, a one-room schoolhouse also towed in and restored complete with outhouse, and a stone building identified by a sign as the smokehouse, but the bars set into its stone windows suggest the building might once have been used for something other than drying meat.

A man dressed in "Indian gear" (strips of fur woven into his hair, a buckskin shirt and odd pants styled to resemble chaps, but cut from a stiff feltlike material) refused to accept the sign's identification of the building's function:

"This place was awfully big for a smokehouse. I mean, if you consider the average person would eat 175 pounds of meat a year, and they would put up enough for six months at a time, well a family of twelve would have needed about twelve hundred pounds for six months. That's not much meat, certainly not enough to fill this place. I saw an old smokehouse down in Boerne, and it was big, but this one is twice the size of that one. This building's just about the right size to have been a Sunday house, I mean a real one."

On the porch of the *fachwork* cabin, I passed a Mexican band playing guitars and singing in Spanish. I was on my way to the Baptist church, which now also serves as the historical society's main center of activities. From inside the auditorium of the church, where they were honoring descendants of ten pioneer families, I heard the sound of applause. I didn't join the crowd there, but stopped to talk to the women displaying their hand-weavings in an adjacent room.

One woman, Sarah Austin, said she had moved to Fredericksburg from San Antonio after her husband retired from the Air Force, and now she is active in a local circle of women who gather together for handcrafts. She sat over a beautiful piece of green lace that she was tatting with a long needle, and explained the dyed yarn samples she had laid out before her on the table.

"These were done with yellow onion peels," she said and showed me three rich shades of yellow and yellow-brown. "This one was made with pecans."

"You mean just the shells, or the whole nut?"

"The entire thing. You know, when a pecan's growing it has several stages, and I use them when they are still green, when the shells haven't hardened yet. And this one's dyed with coffee, just regular coffee like you'd buy in the store. There's one around here I dyed with tea."

"You mean regular tea, like Lipton's or something?"

"Here it is. Yes, as a matter of fact this one *was* Lipton's. And this one's dandelion. And here's blackberry."

"I understand that the cochineal insect grows around here," I said, remembering a fact I'd read when I tried to teach myself to weave on a backstrap loom while I lived in Fredericksburg a few years ago. "Do you ever use that to make red dye?"

"No. I have dogs that drink out of every puddle that gathers anywhere, so I use only natural things and alum."

"Because you don't want to poison your dogs?"

"And I only use things that are biodegradable," she continued. "There's only one commercial dye I'll use," she showed me a large tapestry she was weaving onto a netted cloth with a needle—the orange and yellow hues vibrant in a floral pattern. "It's from Australia, but completely biodegradable. But is it expensive! Worth it, but expensive."

"How's the lightfastness of these natural dyes?" I asked, and she paused a moment to think.

"The onion is good. And the pecan and coffee. The others are a little less good, like, for example, the blackberry tends to fade a bit."

"Do you have blackberry brambles?" I asked. "I didn't realize they grow around here. Last summer I was in Oregon when the blackberries were ripe and I made jam with them."

"Oh yes, I've got blackberries in my yard. Last year I picked eighty-seven gallons. Most of it I use to make wine, and I make it the old way, like my grandparents made it. I don't put any sulfites or any of that kind of stuff in it."

"Are there any tricks, any harvesting aids you can use to gather them?" I remembered being poked and prodded by blackberry thorns.

"I just wear a pair of gloves, regular rubber gloves like you'd use to wash dishes. You still have to be careful about the thorns, though."

Sarah lives in a big rock house in the country outside Stonewall with her husband, Alan. Alan likes to garden, she said when I asked what kept him occupied while she tatted, knitted, and wove.

"We grow most of our own vegetables," she said. "And we don't use anything but a little Sevin dust and some Roundup."

Like several people I overheard conversing throughout the day, we discovered that we are probably distantly related through our kinship networks in the New Braunfels area.

"Small world," she observed. "I worked for a long time in a secretarial pool in San Antonio, and I liked seeing people all the time. I miss that a little, but I also like to have my privacy. Living out here I get to have it both ways for the most part," she said, and told me to visit her and her husband at their home.

3. The Village Blacksmith

Early History: Among the group were expert craftsmen, farmers, mechanics, tradesmen, gunsmiths, professional men, a few nobles, and sturdy women of courage and ingenuity, skilled in the household arts—all dauntless, self-reliant, thrifty, industrious, God-fearing folk, determined to establish permanent homes for themselves and their posterity in a land of political, economic and religious freedom and opportunity.

Fredericksburg Chamber of Commerce, *Fredericksburg: In the Texas Hill Country*

Blacksmith shops were as important, and almost as abundant, in pioneer days as garages and filling stations are now. . . . Modern "children coming home from school" in a big yellow bus are missing something thrilling when they can no longer stop and "look in at the open door," as Longfellow put it, and watch a blacksmith beat a hot bar of iron into the contours of a horseshoe or see the "mighty man" sharpen a plowshare by beating a keen edge on it.

Gilbert J. Jordan, *Yesterday in the Texas Hill Country*

The Kammlah house and barn are full now of the accumulated antique wealth of the historical society preserved under glass and behind signs that read, "Please Do Not Touch the Exhibits." Inside the barn a woman in her fifties pointed to a piece of wooden equipment sitting in a corner and asked me, "What is that, can you tell me? I think my grandfather had one, but I can't remember what it was used for."

I looked at the machine, with its wooden wheel on one side that must have been a place for a pulley attachment. My uncle told me they used to run a belt from the engine of a Model T to the sausage grinder to cut down on work, and this set-up looks like a similar arrangement. On top sat a bin which might have been used to funnel something into a place where I could see metal teeth set into a wooden cylinder. I had absolutely no idea what that something must have been, so the woman asked one of the women tending a craft table to explain what it might have been.

The craftswoman looked for a moment, and she had no more idea about its former purpose than I did.

"Look at this," she said, walking toward another piece of equipment. "It looks like an old ice cream maker." I resisted the urge to say what it really was, a knowledge I had only because I read the attached label a few minutes earlier. "Oh, it's a honey extractor," she said.

Inside the old schoolhouse, a young woman tended a table with bowls of beads set out. For three tickets, children could use the green, red, blue, and black plastic beads to make a bracelet.

"We wanted to use wood beads," the woman explained. "But they're so expensive. One little bead like this is fifty cents. So we just bought the colors that look more like wood."

"What's the 'Children's Discovery Center'?" I asked in reference to the sign on the table.

She explained that the Center conducts programs for children ranging from puppet workshops to field trips to Enchanted Rock.

"Next month we're taking them to Ladybird [a state park on the edge of town] to listen to David McKelvey from over in Ingram. He's an authority on birds. He knows a lot of birds and can do their calls. You've probably seen him; he's been on *The Tonight Show*."

"We moved here a year ago, and I just love it here," she said when I asked whether she has lived in Fredericksburg long. "We moved here because my husband and I wanted to see each other. He was working 70/80 hours a week at computer consulting. We came because we wanted him to work less, and me to get a chance to do something besides just stay at home. Now we both teach at ACC [Austin Community College]. They just started here last year. There are a lot of newcomers here, and they're the ones who don't want it to change. The old-timers can't wait for the city things to get here, and the newcomers all say, 'No, that's what we came here for, to get away from all that.'"

When a group of children came in to make bracelets, I moved on to the lean-to added to the side of the barn. There, a thirtyish man worked at a blacksmith forge, and as people filtered in and out, their children (boys only, I noticed that the parents held their little girls back) took turns cranking the handle that produces air to fan the forge's heat. The man pulled a cast-iron rod from the forge and pounded its end into a point. He explained his trade to the group of people watching him. He told a story about his grandfather:

> He was a shipsmith on a ship that carried livestock from Angus County, Ireland, to New York and Texas. What they would do is put the cows in manacles, with their heads held tight so they couldn't all move to one side and tip the ship over. When a cow died they would pull it out and put a spacer in to keep them in place. There was always plenty of fresh meat on those ships, since the loss rate was around 60 percent or more. Sometimes they would get to the end of trip, which didn't take long—only about a year or so—with only ten or eleven cows. My grandfather made twelve trips to pay for the passage of his family to the United States. It was his job to maintain and repair the manacles.

"Why didn't they just bring young calves," one woman asked, "so they could carry more?"

"That's a good question," the blacksmith replied, "but the problem with young calves is that they need to be let out to nurse, and they died more easily, so in the long run it made more sense to bring young, but full-grown cows, and a few big bulls."

"Have you lived in Fredericksburg all your life?" I asked during a lull in the eddies of people flowing into the shed.

"I moved here about six years ago from Corpus Christi."

"Were you a blacksmith there? Why'd you move here?"

"I had a welding supply company there, but I just decided that money wasn't the main thing in life. I came here because you can pursue other things. People move here because they want the opportunity to live a simpler life, or a more spiritual life. It's not because of money."

A new group of people had knotted themselves in the doorway of the shed, and the blacksmith again started the process of explaining his work while I walked toward the main part of the museum inside the old house.

4. Elaine Schelling

"German houses stand for something we all want today," observed one Anglo traveler through Texas in the 1980s. "They represent solid-ity, stability, surety. They are close to nature. These are things we have forgotten today."

> Glen E. Lich, "Rural Hill Country," in *Eagle in the New World:*
> *German Immigration to Texas and America*

The back room of the Kammlah house has been opened up to make room for a long display case down the center. By the time I finally found my way inside, the room was stuffy with the accumulated heat of bod-ies passing through all day, and the woman acting as docent for the room, Elaine, looked warm and tired. She was talking to a visitor about her own German background.

"We're coming to find out more and more about the way we were watched during the Second World War," she said. "My grandfather es-caped from the Kaiser's army during the first war, and somehow they found out. We're finding out that our family was pretty closely watched after that."

"How are you discovering this?" I eagerly interrupted, then realized my curiosity made me sound as if I was participating in the surveillance myself.

"Well, friends who go to Washington say they've seen things in files there," she said. "I can't remember a specific example right now, but the evidence is there."

The other visitors went on to the next room, so I moved closer to the docent. She had a non-Texas accent, so I explained my interest in understanding why people choose to live in Fredericksburg.

"We discovered Fredericksburg in the early seventies," Elaine said. "It was 1973, and we were on our way to San Antonio, and we spent the night in Fredericksburg. And it was dark when we got here. The next morning we were wandering around, and we just fell in love with the town, and I said to my husband, 'This is where I want to live when we retire.' And retirement was such a long time off at that time. And we'd make several trips down here. Each time we came, we liked it more. There's an ambience here. The people are friendly. It's youth oriented, and you can pick up on that just in the trips you make to town."

"It's 'youth oriented'? What do you mean?"

"Well, like in 1991, I believe it was, or '92, we got a brochure from Fredericksburg Independent School District, and in it, it showed the number of scholarships, and there was almost a quarter of a million dollars in scholarships for the graduating seniors from the local merchants. And you don't find that in just any town. When our boys were growing up, and they were in Little League, just the parents would go out to watch them play, and in this town, everybody shows up for Little League."

"The scholarship thing is kind of a double-edged sword, though," I observed. "Because they give all that money and these kids go away to school. A lot of them don't want to or can't come back to make a living here like they used to."

"Well, I've made a lot of friends here, and if you own a business in town, you can still go to college and you come back, and you use your business experience and you stay here. And if you don't have a business in town—and this happens with a lot of them, and you find this even with the docents here [at the museum]—they will move away. They will go to places like San Antonio, Austin, Houston, Dallas, Fort Worth, but they will maintain their property in Fredericksburg, or around Fredericksburg. They come down periodically to check on it, make sure everything's okay. And when they retire, they come back here to Fredericksburg."

"Yeah, I was talking to Mr. Kaseri outside, and he did that."

"So did the Wagners," she said. "She's a docent, and he's been patrolling the grounds. The Schimmermans did that. A lot of the people, you know, didn't own their own business. Now Madelaine and Ted Williams have their own business, so they stayed here, and they haven't hardly traveled anywhere. They're very content—well, of course, I'm very content to stay here too—it's added twenty years to my life. This is a slow, easy way of life. People are friendly. It's not very expensive to live here. The cost of living is much less than other places."

"So you moved here in '73?"

"No, we moved here in '90, after we retired."

"Oh, I see, but you first saw it in '73?"

"In '73. We kept coming back. One year my husband asked me what I wanted for my birthday, and I said, 'I want a trip to Fredericksburg.' And that's what I got! So we're always discovering new things. We knew we were going to retire in this town."

"How did you start making friendships here? Obviously you must have made friends here before you moved here?"

"No, didn't know a soul when we came here. I'm fascinated with history. I love history, and I signed up as a volunteer with the historical society. And I studied the history of it. Texas history, U.S. history, and Fredericksburg history is very fascinating. I'm still learning a lot, but the more I learn, the more I like it. Because we've kept our German traditions in this town. And then, what holds true today is pretty much what held true when the settlers came. For instance, St. Mary's Catholic Church was the first church with a denomination that was built here. But it wasn't built just by the German Catholics; it was built by all the community. The same way with the first Lutheran church. And the first Methodist church. The whole town pitched in. And today, well St. Mary's has its Mayfest—the Maifest, they call it—coming up this month, and the whole town goes to it. They're just so community minded here. They support all the projects like that. Oktoberfest. Kristkindl Market. And then, of course, we've got the oldest established county fair in the state of Texas here. I love to go to that. I love to look at the cattle that are on display there."

"Did you move up here onto a ranch, or a farm, into the country?"

"No, we moved *from* the country, actually. We're too old to keep up with five acres of fire ants, so we gave up. We bought a lot in town so we don't have to fight them so hard. That's hard work fighting those fire ants."

"Yeah, I know, I know. My uncle's got a piece of property down around Kendalia, and I go down there, I've put a small garden in down there, and the fire ants are awful."

"They drove me out of my garden," she said.

"So what does your husband do around here? You're out here volunteering to do this . . . " She pointed at a man standing nearby, "—this is your husband?"

"That's my husband," she said.

"Hello," I said.

"I was just waiting to see if she was going to tell any lies about me," said her husband, Alan. "Yeah, it's hell with those ants. You have to put so much poison down. If you don't keep at it constantly, they'll just overwhelm you."

"Is there a Gillespie County [agricultural] extension office where you can get fire ant stuff cheaply?" I asked. "I know they have it over in Comal County."

"Yeah, a lot of counties have that, but I really don't know, I haven't checked on it here."

"I'm going to let the two of you talk," Elaine said and left the room.

"I have a tape recorder going here," I said. "Do you mind if I keep that going while we talk a little bit."

"No, that's fine. I don't know as much as my wife does about all this," Alan said and waved an arm at a display case full of antiques.

"That's all right, I'm not interested in just this kind of history," I said. "She was telling me a little bit of your own history, about why you came here. I don't know if you heard this before, but I'm a graduate student at Rice in Houston, doing my dissertation research up here, and one of the things I'm studying is why people come here, and why they want to stay. What makes it feel like home to them."

"Yeah, well, I grew up on a farm in Illinois, and I worked, well I worked for thirty-five years with American Airlines in various jobs. And I spent eleven years in the New York area, which I didn't like. I think the main trouble with that part of the country is it's overcrowded. When you get in a big city, they're so crowded, and your transportation's difficult.

And people begin to sort of . . . not think of each other as neighbors, you know. It's all push and shove."

"Houston, where I went to school, seems like that."

"I got a transfer to Texas, and I worked in the learning center there, and that's where I retired from in Fort Worth. And then we lived there for a few years after I retired, and then we moved here. Which means getting back to basics, I guess. It's always felt best to me to be in a smaller town, or the country. The style of living's simpler. This town fit in with most of our ideas of a place to retire. Not to go to Florida or Arizona or something. We like to be among real people, not just all senior citizens. Although we do have a lot here."

"Yeah, I've noticed that. A lot of people I've been talking to are older people, retired."

"And a lot of people move here for a very good reason. They have an excellent school."

"The school system's good here?" I asked.

"I guess it has a good reputation to be a good place to live. As a matter of fact, there was a national study made, designed to see where were the best places to retire. And out of ten, I think this was five or six, which I couldn't hardly believe."

"In the nation?"

"Yeah, it's really hard to believe," Alan said. "But if you put it all together, I think it fits pretty well."

Houses and Homes, Building and Dwelling

The house, in the words of a German scholar, "is the embodiment of a people's soul." Especially is this true of houses built by immigrants settling in a new cultural and physical environment. Observe closely the homes of such uprooted people and you will obtain a visual statement of the immigrants' attitudes toward their Old World cultural heritage and the alien host culture surrounding them, of acculturation and the possibility of eventual assimilation. True, the folk house permits a posthumous look into the very heart of the immigrant. When viewed from this perspective, the nineteenth-century dwellings erected by German colonists in the Texas Hill Country are most instructive. What house architecture emerged from this curious confluence of peoples, this juxtaposition and interplay of Teutonic peasant, Anglo frontiersman, and Mexican peon? And what does the resultant domestic architecture tell us about the early German experience in the Texas hills?

Terry G. Jordan, "German Folk Houses in the Texas Hill Country,"
in *German Culture in Texas*

In Fredericksburg the houses are stone,
they remind me of wristwatches, glass polished,
years ticking by in each wall.
I don't like stone, says one. What if it fell?
I don't like Fredericksburg, says the other.
Too many Germans driving too slow.
She herself is German as Stuttgart.
The day presses forward wearing complaints,
charms on its bony wrist.

Naomi Shihab Nye, "Going for Peaches,
Fredericksburg, Texas"

1. The Well-Digger's House

During the first period I lived in Fredericksburg, I rented a small cottage a few miles outside town. The cottage had been built in the 1970s on a piece of property that had contained an old stone barn and the burned-out shell of a stone house. The people who bought the property, a somewhat affluent couple from outside the region, had gone to great lengths to rebuild the house and furnish it with old pie safes, beds, and other antiques. It was actually far too small a structure for their family, so they turned the barn into a combination living area/sleeping dormer for the children. A swimming pool and the cottage I rented (built to house an adult daughter for a few years) completed a roughly square domestic compound.

Even if I wanted to, I probably could not number the works that have been written, painted, sketched, and photographed using the limestone architecture of Fredericksburg and the surrounding German-settled farmsteads as subject matter. Local history books, scholarly studies, and nearly countless paintings and photographic representations attest to the staying power and interest generated by these old stone houses.

What is it about these buildings that captures people's imaginations? What kinds of things do they represent to contemporary minds? Why do so many people want not only to see them but—as evidenced by hugely inflated property values in Fredericksburg and the surrounding Hill Country—buy them, renovate them, occupy them, and merge (in their own minds at least) their life histories with those of the builders of these usually simple structures?

One man I talked to was painstakingly restoring a stone house in town that had belonged to a well-digger. I stopped to watch him work one day when I was out for a walk, and he took me inside to show me what he was doing.

"This house is completely the opposite of the house where I live in Houston," he told me while we looked at the small sleeping loft and the kitchen he was slowly installing in one corner of the high-ceilinged main floor. "That house—it's a suburban home built in the sixties—was made as quickly and as cheaply as it could be made. And you feel it when you walk through it. It's like the walls are hardly even there." He runs a hand gently along the stone, as he leads me out the back door to show me the work he is doing on the patio. "The original kitchen was a lean-to just added to the back here. We tore that down, but the old well's still here." He shows me the wellcap he's put on. "That well was hand-dug. The guy who built this house was a well-digger. That's how he made his living. He actually died by falling into one of the wells he was digging." This man was retiring soon, and planned to move with his wife to this building. "It would never have been big enough for us and all of our kids. But they're already asking when they get to come and visit us here. They love this house already. Maybe more than they ever loved any of the houses where we lived when they were growing up."

Is a house simply a structure meant to keep the elements off our heads? The essayist Scott Russell Sanders gives the etymology:

> The word *house* derives from an Indo-European root meaning to cover or conceal. I hear in that etymology furtive, queasy undertones. Conceal from what? From storms? beasts? enemies? from the eye of God? *Home* comes from a different root meaning "the place where one lies." That sounds less fearful to me. . . . However leaky or firm, whether tar paper or brick, the shell of a house gives only shelter; a home gives sanctuary. (Sanders 1993, 29–30)

That's a somewhat ingenuous line of questioning, because of course a house *is* meant for the basic need of shelter, but both the man renovating the well-digger's house and the essayist in this quotation seem to be suggesting that "house" and "home" are not synonymous.

2. Home in Impermanence

I have two friends who live, when they're not following the apple or blueberry harvests, in a basket in the north woods of Michigan. They dug a hole in the ground, then used saplings bent to form an arched structure, and constructed the walls by weaving still smaller saplings in and out like a basket. After that, they covered the structure with thick plastic, burlap, and some carpet remnants they salvaged from a renovation project in Marquette. The whole thing is banked over with earth. I've only seen pictures and heard them describe the process of building what he calls "the wig-thing," and she calls her "womb-room." They say that with the woodstove going, it gets so warm in there in the winter, despite weeks of subzero weather outside, that they can hardly stand to be in there, and they have to go out for frequent cross-country ski trips to cool off.

I'll repeat a quotation I used earlier as an epigraph:

"German houses stand for something we all want today," observed one Anglo traveler through Texas in the 1980s. "They represent solidity, stability, surety. They are close to nature. These are things we have forgotten today." (Lich 1986, 45)

Solidity. Stability. Surety. Closeness to nature.

The basket-house of my friends measures up only on this last point. But it seems clear, when I listen to them talk about the place they've made for themselves, that despite the ephemeral nature of their building materials, the act of living in that house invites an opportunity for dwelling that few contemporary houses offer to the people seeking shelter inside their framed-in walls of sheetrock, toxic adhesives, and two-by-fours.

3. The New House Next Door

CAUTION: CONTAINS TOULENE, HEXANE, AND PETROLEUM NAPHTHA. May cause eye, skin, nose and throat irritation. May affect the brain and nervous system causing dizziness, headache or nausea. Using this product will expose you to toulene which is known to the State of California to cause birth defects or other reproductive harm.

Label of DAP 4000 Subfloor Adhesive

Building and thinking are, each in its own way, inescapable for dwelling. The two, however, are also insufficient for dwelling so long as each busies itself with its own affairs in separation instead of listening to one another . . . the *real plight of dwelling* does not lie merely in the lack of houses . . . what if humanity's homelessness consisted in this, that human beings still do not even think of the *real* plight of dwelling as *the* plight. (italics in original)

Martin Heidegger, "Building Dwelling Thinking,"
in *Poetry, Language, Thought*

From inside the foundation of the new house being built on the lot next door to my rented apartment I sit watching a thunderstorm approach from the north to replace the steady light of the stars and the half-moon with sudden bursts of lightning. Sitting in the dirt, I smell freshly sawn pine boards and see the squat shapes of poured-concrete footings that will provide support for the house's floor. Scattered around me are empty tubes of plastic adhesive that the workers used this afternoon to glue the long boards together.

This house is being built by successive teams of workers. Like a relay race in which the baton is the only thing that will travel the entire distance, these inanimate boards and concrete will be the only things that are present for the entire life of the house. The future owner, who lives now in a city hundreds of miles away, has seen only floor plans and drawings. When the house was begun, a Mexican American man and a Native American man set up the forms for the concrete under the watchful eye of an older man, clearly a foreman of some sort. When the forms were ready, another Mexican American man arrived driving a cement truck. The foreman directed the gutter of the mixer to fill the forms while the two others troweled the surfaces smooth.

I haven't seen those people in several days now. The next phase of construction is being done by two young men who seem to be relatives to one another. They are sawing and gluing boards that will reach across the entire foundation and rest on the hardened barrels of concrete dotted inside the square of the outer wall. One of these men explained to me that this house will cost more than a hundred thousand dollars—not much by urban standards, but in this small rural community, that seems nearly enough to build a university. He said it is being built to resemble, at least in facade, the old limestone and metal-roofed houses put up over the last century and a half by German settlers and their descendants.

On Sunday, several elderly couples from the neighborhood visited the site, pointing out various aspects of the building to one another. They are curious about the floor plan, and about the person who will soon live in their midst.

As I sit inside the foundation and watch the lightning streaks in the sky, I am wondering about the way this place is being built. Homes in this area used to be made by the people who planned to live in them. They would often get help from their neighbors, but the group doing the building always included somebody who was going to live inside the walls being erected. This was, at the time, a matter of necessity, but it also says something about the nature of the dwelling that was to occur. You didn't let others build your home for you; you had to make the place with your own hands as well as with the hands of your neighbors. It was an act of "ownness," of making something your own.

This kind of communal building still occasionally occurs around here. A small church at the edge of town, for example, was put up over one weekend by the entire church community. In the contemporary United States, however, construction of the buildings we are going to try to make into homes and dwelling places is usually left to architects and construction workers, "experts" in the field.

This might be seen simply as a matter of convenience—who today has the time or knowledge to build his/her own dwelling place?—but I'm convinced that there is something more here. How many of us know how to make a home, both in the sense of building the structure and in the sense of making that structure habitable, a place full of dwelling?

When one landscape architect set out to explore this question, he found people often could not make a place comfortable enough for them to feel "at home." Even a person trained as an interior designer, a profession that attempts to make the inside of a structure into a home, was unable to make the *space* of his house into the *place* of home. The words "space" and "place" have recently become fashionable, and have served a variety of meanings for different writers. I understand "space" as general and abstract, a form of distancing from the world, while "place" is particular and concrete, a landscape inhabited by body and mind. Here is a description of this interior designer's experience:

> Robert, an interior designer, was at the time of the interview troubled over his discontent with a house he and his wife had been living in for a year. Despite his profession, he had found it seemingly impossible to create a comfortable home. Indeed, the layout of the house made this very difficult: the largest central room which was both entry hall and living room had no less than seven door openings off it. He and his wife were forever leaving the house—to go on trips, to go biking or hiking, to go out to eat or for entertainment. Robert wanted to spend more time at home, but the reason he did not do so was a mystery to him. (Marcus 1992, 106)

I have a friend whose family lives in exactly this sort of structure in Houston. There are five doorways in the central living space, and when I visit this friend, we are forever trying to find an intimate place in the house where we can talk undisturbed. We almost always end up opting for a walk around the neighborhood. The street, ironically, provides a more habitable place than the house itself.

What do these things have to do with the house that a whole task force of workers is putting up next door to my small apartment?

I am asking questions about the nature of a world in which houses are prepared for us like packages, without our aid or consideration. What kind of home will be built of boards that are glued together using a material that has been deemed deadly to infants and others? I remember reading a poem that said something like: "Blessed is the day when a new household takes its place among the myriads of homes in the world." But how blessed, how thoughtful, how homelike, is a structure that rests on the labor of invisible and forgotten workers whose names the house owner will never know?

Remaining, Returning, and Re-placing

> . . . if every American is several people, and one of them is or would like to be a placed person, another is the opposite, the displaced person, cousin not to Thoreau but to Daniel Boone, dreamer not of

Walden Ponds but of far horizons, traveler not in Concord but in wild unsettled places, explorer not inward but outward. Adventurous, restless, seeking, asocial or antisocial, the displaced American persists by the million long after the frontier has vanished. He exists to some extent in all of us, the inevitable by-product of our history: the New World transient.

Wallace Stegner, "The Sense of Place," in *Where the Bluebird Sings to the Lemonade Springs*

Then there's the group of people who've been here forever. They make up a very large part of the community. A lot of young people leave, but at some point many of them seem to come back. People tend to stay on the farm or work the ranches they've worked for years.

Leo Tynan, a Fredericksburg doctor, quoted in "The Land, The Roots, the Myth," *Texas Monthly*, March 1990

Fredericksburg is a comfortable sort of town, if you can adjust to the highway lined with tourist shops that used to be just a main street. Now it's both a major thoroughfare for westbound truck drivers and a daytime boutique where you can buy everything from smoked ham to mountain dulcimers, with Indian nostalgia, Guatemalan fabrics, baseball cards, African furniture, and early American antiques thrown in on the side. The population is large enough to make privacy possible, yet there are few enough residents that if you walk down the street (on a relatively tourist-free day) you'll see many faces that you recognize, and most people greet you with a smile, wave, or nod of the head.

The people of the town are mainly of three sorts: descendants of the settlers who originally came into the hills in the nineteenth century, and who have always lived in the area—they're called "natives" around here, though anybody over fifty or sixty years old in this group is also called an "old-timer"; people born and/or raised here who moved away for a significant period of their lives and later returned; and people who moved from elsewhere but wish they'd been born here themselves.

I'm going to call these respective groups "those who remained," "those who returned," and "those who re-placed." The re-placed are often the most vocal about the area's unique qualities as a place, and they also sometimes take over the places of original owners and community leaders.

My father's people settled in the Hill Country south of here with the earliest immigrants, but as I've already said, we spent most of my growing up moving around, and I was actually born in Nebraska, so I guess I'm as much a "wish I'd been" as I am a "native," with the added complication that I've returned to a place where I lived before. If there's anything like a borderland between the three groups I'm talking about, then I'm placed squarely in the gateway at the fenceline.

By regional standards, Fredericksburg is an old place, and it is largely this age and the old buildings that remain in use that have made the town so attractive to tourists, travelers, and prospective immigrants. One Connecticut man, a painter, who moved to town more than twenty years ago, told me: "I'd never seen a place where the buildings looked so old. I mean, I came out here from Connecticut, where we had houses from 1694 beautifully kept up, but what struck me here was how everything looked so primitive. The people who built here had to work this place with their bare hands. They built with what they had."

Those Who Remained

1. Denise

Wherever she is, whoever she is, the rural woman in Texas has experienced changes in her lifestyle that would have amazed her grandmother. These changes are the result of the impact of rural electrification, modern technology, improved transportation, mass media and education.

Martha Mitten Allen, "Women on the Land," in *Texas Country: The Changing Rural Scene*

Intrinsic to any tradition that spans several generations, grandmothers to granddaughters, is a difficulty of identifying what a German-Texan is, to say nothing of what a German-Texan woman is.

Dona Reeves-Marquardt, "Tales of the Grandmothers: Women as Purveyors of German-Texan Culture I," in *Eagle in the New World: German Immigration to Texas*

When I first lived in Fredericksburg I volunteered a few times to work at the library. One day I sat at the reference desk and tried to help people find information about local history. The irony was palpable—I was an outsider who knew almost nothing about the town's history, at least nothing more than what I might have gleaned from reading a few local histories of German immigration to the Hill Country. When someone asked me a question I couldn't help them with, I sent them downstairs to the main desk. At the time, I simply sent them there, because I knew no alternative. I assumed someone at the desk would be able to tell them the proper place to look.

I know now that I sent those history seekers to a good place. Several of the women who work at the library have lived in Fredericksburg all their lives. Denise, for example, was born and raised here, and has worked at the library for many years.

While I stood at the checkout desk one day, Denise told me she has been married twice, the first time to the son of a solidly entrenched German family. Her own family is an equally rooted German one. Her first marriage ended, however, and she has since married a Mexican American man.

"My family doesn't like it, of course," she said. "My grandmother, my mother, my sisters, none of them really want to have anything to do with my husband. I guess I've always been the one who was different. I was the one who always wanted to move away, though I never got the chance. And I'm the one who avoided many of my family's prejudices."

I told her my story about applying for work at a local turkey plant and discovering the racism latent in the plant manager's attitude.

"Oh, you should talk to my grandparents," she said. "They both worked in that plant for a long time, and they could tell you all kinds of stories. I don't have anything interesting to say," she said. "I've just worked here at the library and had my families."

"Oh, the people who work at the library always know more than they let on," I responded.

2. Lorna and Vivian

In the early days most families had private graveyards near their homes, but after 1900 the rural church cemeteries took their place.

Gilbert G. Jordan, *Yesterday in the Texas Hill Country*

. . . *Campo santo,* they call it,
holy field, and even those without belief

say it is blessed by the dead who lie there,
because, surely, all of them were loved once
by someone. Some of them are still remembered.

Susan Wood, "Campo Santo"

On my way to write a letter and get an ice cream at the Dairy Queen, I stop at the cemetery on Baron's Creek to let my dog walk for a while, and to watch the sunset. As I climb out of the truck, I notice a gravestone that reads: "KNEESE" and this catches my eye because earlier this afternoon I rode my bike into the hills surrounding town and spent a long time soaring down the hillsides on Kneese Road. The coincidence seems worth honoring with a closer look at the Kneese graveplot.

While I read the names and dates on the monument, I overhear a conversation between a group of four people tending a nearby plot. They are speaking German, and I get excited because this will perhaps give me a chance to practice the lessons I have been listening to on tapes. But they speak quickly, comfortable in a language that comes off my tongue sounding as I were trying to swallow rocks at the same time as speaking. I can't understand a word.

My dog wanders over and promptly attacks the man's shoes, and the people pause in their conversation to look at the puppy.

"Abbie," I say, "Don't eat that man's shoes!"

"I didn't see you there," says one of the women. "I just saw the puppy."

"He's taking me for a walk," I say.

The man and one of the women say good-bye to the other two women, and they beat a hasty retreat from my dog's attention. The remaining two ogle the puppy, and we talk about the breed—Australian Shepherd—for a few minutes. One of the women had such a dog for a while herself.

"But I had to get rid of him," she says while she strokes Abbie's back. "He got too big for me."

I walk around to the front of the plot, and ask how the women are related to the people buried there. All three of the burials have dates in the 1930s.

"Well, she's my sister," one of the women says and points to the other woman, who has taken a handful of pulled weeds to the garbage can. "And this is our mother," she says and points to one of the names on the monument. "And that's her sister. And our father, too. I'm not quite sure why our mother's sister got buried here, but there she is."

They go on with their business, and I sit down on a low wall nearby to watch them pull weeds and chop at the roots with a hoe.

"It looks great," I say. "Are you going to plant anything in the dirt?"

"We want to put down concrete," one of the sisters says. "And then put gravel over the top like these other graves." She points to a neighboring plot.

"But flowers seem more appropriate," I suggest.

"Well, but it's so much work. We can't hardly keep up with it anymore. We tried to get some of our cousins, who are a lot younger, to help out, but they're so busy, so many things to do nowadays, that they don't have time."

"They used to keep the place up so nice," the other sister says. "There was an old man who had a sort of retarded son . . . he was retarded wasn't he?" The first sister nods. "They used to be at it all day, even in the heat, and they kept this whole place cleaned up."

"'Course, it was a lot smaller then," the other sister observes.

"You're from around here, then?" I ask. "You've been around long enough to see these changes?"

"We've been here all our lives. You might say we're 'natives.'"

"Seems to be something rare around here," I say. "Most of the people I talk to moved in from someplace else."

"Oh yes, there's a lot of that here now. Lots of people moving in."

"What do you think about that? What do you think about the way that's changed things here?"

"Well, I think it's a good thing," one sister says. "They've restored so many of the buildings, and they're preserving them. The town looks like . . . well, it looks like you would think a small town ought to look like."

"That's what everybody says to me," I say. "They say that's why they moved here."

"Well," she says, "if I weren't from here, and I was thinking about visiting a town, I guess Fredericksburg would be like the town I would imagine visiting."

"I'm not like her," the other sister disagrees and goes on pulling weeds. "I don't like it the same as her. Things have changed too much."

I explain that I'm in town writing about exactly these kinds of things, about the way people think about what Fredericksburg is. One of them asks where I'm from.

"Well, my father's people are from south of here, around Kendalia," I say, conscious that I am telling my life story in a particular way. I've stopped being vague when people ask, and start with my father's family, then move on to my mother's. Only if the conversation goes on for a while do I mention that I've moved a lot, so while I've lived in a number of places, I'm *from* none of them, or maybe I'm from all of them.

Then I tell the sisters a story about Uncle Herbert attending the anniversary of Father Hildebrandt, a relative of mine who served as the pastor of the Catholic church in Fredericksburg for a long time.

"Oh yes!" says one of the sisters. "He was a good man."

They go on pulling weeds and avoiding ants.

"What do you know about Father Hildebrandt?" I ask, trying to keep a conversation going.

"Well," says the sister who had commented about Father Hildebrandt's goodness, "we're not Catholics, so we didn't know him well, but we heard he was a good man."

"If you're writing about the history here, you must have seen that angel over there," one of the women says; and when I say that I haven't, she says, "Oh, but you have to see that. It's an Elisabet Ney, so you should see it."

(Elisabet Ney was a mid-nineteenth-century sculptor who was famous for her time. She moved to Texas from Germany. Her studio was in Austin, where she did sculptures of many of Texas's early leaders. Today her former studio has been turned into a museum.)

"It's over there," the other sister says and waves. "It's an angel sort of leaning on its hands, and you should see the fingers. She made them in detail. It's beautiful."

"I'll have to walk over and look," I say. "It's over there?"

"I'll see if I can find it," says one of the sisters as she starts walking toward the center of the graveyard.

"Show him, Vivian," says the other sister. "He needs to see that."

I follow Vivian through the cemetery. She says, "It's here somewhere in the middle of one of these wrought-iron graveplots."

We look together until she says, "There it is!"

We walk over and look at the monument. It is made of white marble, but most of the stone has discolored to black with age. She calls my attention to the fingers.

"They're very intricate," I say. "And the eyes are something to look at."

"Do you know Jeeper Collins?" she asks.

"I know that he's a jeweler in town," I say. "But that's all."

"Well, Jeeper's related to this woman, Schlierrer. By marriage, I guess. I think his wife was a Schlierrer. Anyway, he made a necklace with that on it." She points to the angel.

"You mean a cameo or something like that?" I ask.

"Yes. And a pair of earrings with that angel on it too. I'm not exactly sure how he's related, but anyway, he made that necklace."

My dog comes bounding over from where he's been tormenting the other sister in her efforts to tend the graveplot.

"I guess I'd best get back to helping Lorna before she says I'm always lazying my way out of work," Vivian says as she goes back through the field of gravestones to her task of tending to the graves of the past.

3. Terry

As the Texas Germans gained control of their environment they began to build after their own temperament and German traditions, and some of the houses they built in the better times of those earlier years still stand as monuments to one of the main characteristics of German buildings, the sense of permanence.

Francis Edward Abernathy, "Deutschtum in Texas: A Look at Texas-German Folklore," in *German Culture in Texas*

The nature of building is letting dwell. Building accomplishes its nature in the raising of locations by the joining of their spaces. *Only if we are capable of dwelling, only then can we build.* Let us think for a while of a farmhouse in the Black Forest, which was built some two hundred years ago by the dwelling of peasants. Here the self-sufficiency of the power to let earth and heaven, divinities and mortals enter *in simple oneness* into things, ordered the house. It placed the farm on the wind-sheltered mountain slope looking south, among the meadows close to the spring. . . . A craft which, itself sprung from dwelling, still uses its tools and frames as things, built the farmhouse. Only if we are capable of dwelling, only then can we build. (italics in original)

Martin Heidegger, "Building Dwelling Thinking,"
in *Poetry, Language, Thought*

What does it mean to dwell? Is it simply to find yourself at home somewhere? But what is this "at home"? The dwelling usually experienced as shelter, hearth, comfort, soon takes on an enigmatic aspect when these unusual questions are asked. Is it a kind of spatial excrescence of the human subject? A shell? A more elementary relation with a place? A root? Yet, despite these current and quite reassuring metaphors, the "at home" cannot be reduced to the simple fact of living in symbiosis with a space become familiar, nor even of finding oneself thereby ensconced in a certain soil, linked by a network of bonds and attachments to a land, to a country. "To dwell" also means "to last."

Michel Haar, *The Song of the Earth: Heidegger and the Grounds of the History of Being*

Terry is making a home. He is cutting logs. He is collecting stones. He is raiding dumpsters for useful things. He plans to build a structure that could still be here five hundred years from now. He is gathering pieces of the world to assemble his dwelling place.

Okay. Back up. Get off this galloping rhetorical horse. Terry is a man a few years older than I who is doing something unconventional in contemporary terms—he's building a house using his own time and labor and using the materials available to him from the local environment. This means that he is using a chain saw to cut oak logs and cedar posts off his family's place near Bulverde, Texas; he is scavenging for rocks at a local gypsum mine where they toss aside limestone blocks in order to get at the soft, chalky material that is pressed between paper to make sheetrock drywall; each week he visits the dumpster of a local charity secondhand store in order to reclaim any potentially useful items; he has gathered tons of masonry quality sand from the banks of a local river.

"It's a good time for dumpster diving right now," Terry says. "There's so much wealth flowing into this community because of the tourism and development, and a lot of solid stuff, useable stuff, ends up donated to the hospice. Anything that the old German ladies there don't recognize or that they think won't sell ends up in the dumpster."

I've seen some of his collection. Old quilts, leather clothing, fans, lamps, radios, buckets, hundreds of candles—many items are either new or in fine working condition. He gave me a wool hat made in Nepal that lay in the dumpster and looked like it had never been worn at all.

"Things like the quilts and the leather pieces bother me most," Terry says. "I mean a lot of work went into those quilts, some person spent a lot of time and creativity making those things, and instead of being treasured, they end up dumped out and thrown away. And the leather, the animal products that are still perfectly useful—those come from something that was living, and it seems incredibly wasteful to throw them away when they still have a use and a value."

One day I rode in his battered pickup, which he salvaged from a dump site, to a ranch twenty miles west of Fredericksburg, near Harper, owned by Terry's father. Terry's family lived near Bulverde, at the same time that several generations of my family lived not too far from there. Our families have probably known each other for more than a century, but this was the first significant time we had spent together. We'd had several good conversations sitting in the coffee shop in town, but his personal life seemed guarded by locks to which I did not have the combination. Terry thinks things through carefully. His decisions seem full of the care that my own hurried life often seems to lack.

Terry is building a home; he's slowly gathering together pieces of the world to shape into a home.

"I'm moving pretty slow, and being careful how I think about building this house," Terry says. "To put all this work into building a house and have it not feel right wouldn't be good. I'd like to build something that might still be standing here five hundred years from now."

His building methods are inspired by the centuries-old houses he saw in Germany during two trips he's made to study with master engravers there.

"That just had a profound impact on me. In 1500 those people in that village had already been there at least five hundred years. They had a sense that, 'Here we are; our future generations will be here too, so we might as well build for them.' Here we build disposable houses—fifty to one hundred years is real impermanent in most senses. A friend of mine pointed out that some Indians made decisions based on at least seven generations; that's an awareness of continuity that seems to be lost in the middle of this country's 'me' stuff."

He's been cutting logs at his family's place near Bulverde—big oaks for the walls, cedars for posts, and last week he told me he had just cut six big elms for lumber. One morning he left after our morning visit at a coffee shop to pick up a load of oak lumber, rejects and offcuts from a local hardwoods shop. He bought a lot of usable lumber very cheaply.

"With all the rock houses going up in town, it's a good time for getting extras and offcuts for almost nothing," he says.

Terry's putting together the pieces of this house slowly, a way of letting opportunity unfold on its own, a form of building that echoes with mindfulness and dwelling.

"When I get to thinking how great everything's going, I always pull up short and realize how dangerous what I'm doing could be," he says. "Anything could happen. When I called the guy at the gypsum pit, I told him I'd sign a waiver declaring that I was responsible, and would not hold the quarry liable if anything happened. He thought about it awhile, and finally said, 'I guess you could come out on Sundays when we're not blasting and take whatever you want.' It's still dangerous there. Then, when I'm cutting trees, I mean, anything could happen. So I try not to get too greedy, and remember that while all this stuff I'm gathering is great, I really only have right now to be alive."

Terry's father grudgingly agreed to give up about four acres of ground on the backside of the ranch, with frontage on a county road, for Terry to build a house for himself and his new wife. While we walked around looking at the piece of property, Terry told me about his negotiations with his father.

"When my dad and I were out here trying to establish the boundaries of what he would give me, it was kind of funny. He would step in a few steps to make the piece smaller. Then I'd step out a few steps to make it bigger. It went back and forth like that awhile. My dad has a hard time giving anything up. He's about as self-made as you can get. Comes from a family background of alcoholism and trouble, so he's kind of gotten everything he has by holding onto it with both fists. It's hard for him to let anything go now.

"At first, when I told him I wanted to build out here, he said, 'Well,

I guess I'll give it to you, even though you're not going to do anything to improve the property value.' He's got certain ideas about what's of value, and he thought I was going to build a shack or something. Then, a few weeks ago, he said to me, 'You remember that house you pointed out in Fredericksburg—the one you said you were thinking about building like?' I didn't remember it—it must have been something I said in passing—but he said, 'Well, if you're going to build something like that, you'll really have something. Something valuable.' And him saying that made me realize how, even now, when I'm thirty-six, parental approval still means something to me. It made me feel good to hear him say that."

For Terry, making this home is a process of making whole, of healing past troubles and creating a strong future. Terry has his own business as a fine engraver. His studio and the place where he lives are high-ceilinged rooms above the old variety store in Fredericksburg. He travels to a few festivals each year, including the Texas Folklife Festival in San Antonio, where he demonstrates his craft, and gets customers who commission him to do engraving work for them. Most of his clients are wealthy men from the urban areas of Texas—Houston, Austin, San Antonio, Dallas—who hire him to engrave the metalwork on their favorite rifles or shotguns. He engraves belt buckles, knives, and other objects as well.

At the Folklife Festival one year, Terry met a woman from San Antonio who was intrigued with his work, and they talked for a while. They subsequently began a relationship and are now married and living in several rooms above the variety store. His new wife, whose name is also Terri, turns out to be a relative to me—my "fourth cousin, once removed," as she deciphered based on a genealogical family history written by her grandmother.

Building a house for him and Terri to make into a home is, for Terry, a step toward making a whole, healed life.

Those Who Returned

1. Suzie

Woman's place in the nineteenth century, by contrast with that of the previous century, was based on a philosophic as well as physical commitment to her family. Her days were spent in a continuing and lively participation in the affairs of her husband, children, and relatives and in the care of her household.

> Crystal Sasse Ragsdale, "The German Woman in Frontier Texas,"
> in *Texas: A Free Earth*

Popular images of rural women in Texas are colorful and varied. Rodeo queens and freshly scrubbed 4-H girls flash by in an imaginary parade, while Lady Bird Johnson, Anne Armstrong, and Janie Briscoe pose in rural settings and remind us of their links to the land. "Miss Ellie" Ewing, star of the television series "Dallas," shines brighter than bright, larger than Texas: the Texas Earth Mother who, although part of an immense oil empire, finds meaning in her beloved Southfork ranch. These popular images are attractive and appealing, but are they representative of rural women in Texas today? Who is the rural woman, and how has her life changed in the twentieth century?

> Martha Mitten Allen, "Women on the Land," in *Texas Country:*
> *The Changing Rural Scene*

On my way back home this afternoon, I stopped at the bookstore to look once again at the selection of local and Texas history books. After copying titles into my notebook, I walked toward the door, and commented to the woman who sat behind the counter working on a piece of sewing, "I'm suffering the student's dilemma—too many books, not enough money."

"I'm not a student," she said, "but I know what you mean. Where do you go to school?"

"Rice University, in Houston," I told her. "But I'm living here now to do research."

"What kind of research?"

"Well, usually when people ask me, I tell them I'm interested in why they come here, or why they stay here. Or I tell them that I'm interested in the history of the area. They always tell me about this or that book of local history, or they tell me about one of the historical figures of the town. What I guess I'm really studying, though, is the ways people use that history, why they tell the stories they choose to tell. I think it's part of what makes people want to come here to visit and live."

She looked at me a bit quizzically, as if I'd not quite made sense.

"I'm talking to people who move here from elsewhere, to listen to why they came, and to people who've lived here all their lives, to see why they've stayed, and to people who moved away and came back."

"I've lived here most of my life," she said. "But I moved away for five years, and lived in Edna, Texas. But we didn't like it there."

"Why not? Why did you move back here?"

"We decided we didn't care about making a lot of money, and moved back home where we knew our kids could get a good schooling. Where we knew what things were like."

"How long ago did you move back?"

"We came back about twelve years ago."

"So your children are older, then? Do they still live here?"

"I have one daughter who's twenty and she's married and lives in Austin. And I have a son who's seventeen, and another daughter who's nine.

"How long will you be staying here?" she asked me, and I fumbled for an answer because I don't know how long I will stay, not because my "research" could continue indefinitely, but because I'm not sure I could find a way to support myself in the area.

"That's a real problem," she agreed. "It's hard to find a way to make a living."

"You seem to have found a great way," I observed with a gesture to the bookstore around us.

"Well, it is a great idea, because there aren't any other bookstores here, but I just work here. I don't own the place. I'm a single parent now, so I work here, and then I work at Shearer Publishing during the week. And I also work over in Luckenbach."

"What do you do over there?"

"Oh, I just work in the general store. If you're going to be around for a while, you might drive on down there and see the place."

"I plan to. In fact, I just recently talked to a guy who has family down there, somebody named Burg."

"You mean Bobby?" she asked.

"Yeah, Bobby Burg. He told me I probably shouldn't use his name much around here, because he's got something of a reputation. He's a very funny man."

She laughed.

"Yes, he's funny. He's probably right about not throwing his name around, though. It's interesting what you said about people moving away then coming back, because my daughter always wanted to move away from here. She was in a big hurry to get away, but now she's got a four-month-old baby, and she's talking about moving back. She doesn't want her children exposed to the violence and drugs and stuff in Austin. The baby's small yet, so it will be a while, but my daughter's already talking about moving back."

She told a tantalizing story about her father:

"We're not really German," she said. "But he ran away from home at seven and walked twenty miles to Morris Ranch [a community in Gillespie County] to stay with an old German couple there. When his parents came a few days later to bring him home, he refused to go with them, and the German couple agreed to raise him. He spoke no German at the time, and had to learn the language. He says he nearly forgot how to speak English. My name before I got married was Smith, and when I said I was Suzie Smith from Fredericksburg, people would say, you mean 'Schmidt,' don't you? But I'm not really German."

2. Abel

It is not an unusual life-curve for Westerners—to live in and be shaped by the bigness, sparseness, space, clarity, and hopefulness of the West, to go away for study and enlargement and the perspective that distance and dissatisfaction can give, and then to return to what pleases the sight and enlists the loyalty and demands the commitment.

Wallace Stegner, "Finding the Place: A Migrant Childhood,"
in *Where the Bluebird Sings to the Lemonade Springs*

What invests buildings with life? How do they emerge into the consciousness of people as entities possessing an intangible worth beyond their usefulness or the value of their brick and stone? Is there a basic difference between what they mean to the "informed" architectural expert or conservationist, and what they mean to the people whose lives are interwoven with them?

Tamara Hareven and Randolph Langenbach, "Living Places, Work Places, and Historical Identity," in *Our Past before Us: Why Do We Save It?*

I awoke late in the morning since I'd stayed up late working on a story that is partially fact and partially fiction, and which is set in the countryside near Fredericksburg. After taking a shower I opened the doors in the bathroom that lead to the shopfront that occupies the rooms off Main Street in the place I have temporarily rented. Abel, the carpenter whose name I had been told by my landlord, was standing atop a stepladder and working on the ceiling of one of the rooms of the shop. I'd been told that Abel used to work as an electrical engineer for NASA until he returned to the Hill Country, the area where he grew up, several years ago.

Abel's face is creased and tanned, and his hair is a bit long in back with a bald spot atop his head. He climbed down from the ladder, and we talked while he lit one cigarette after another and squatted in the fluorescent lighting of the room. While we talked about working on these old buildings, Abel drew explanatory diagrams on the two-by-sixes lying by, ready for the repairs. Abel has been a carpenter ever since he returned to Fredericksburg after he "burned out" working for NASA in Houston and Alabama. He prefers doing renovation work on the older buildings in town to working on new houses.

"The old-timers did things differently," he said. "You never know what you're going to find when you tear away the plaster." He pointed to the stripped ceiling of the room where we stood. "Those rafters were just toenailed in. Before I started working here I climbed up on the roof and stood there, and the roof just sagged in, like a bowl, right here where these rafters had been put in." He points at the place above us. "The nails had pulled loose, and this ceiling was just sagging."

We talked about his work on these old buildings, and Abel pointed out that many of the roofs on the oldest buildings in town were steep-pitched, as if they'd been built to throw off heavy snows, snows that never really fall here in Texas.

"It's an example of the way they built what they knew," he says. "'Hans knew vun vay to built,'" he says, affecting a thick German accent in English. "'The vay he learnt in der alt country, and by gott, dat vas the vay he vas going to built.' So you find these pitched roofs built by Hans and the people who learned roofing from him. 'Then the younger volks started getting lazy und builting these flat roofs.'"

"You can read the buildings in this town by looking at the roofs.

You'll see a roof that will have four or five different pitches. A family would build a basic house, then when they needed more space, they'd tack on a porch. Then they'd close that in, and make another porch in another direction. By the time you get to today, standing on some of these roofs is like being on top of a big geometric puzzle with different pieces that don't seem like they should fit together. But it's just the story of the people who lived there."

Abel told me about a job he completed recently on an old house that somebody has converted into a beauty salon.

"The ceiling was all beadboard," he said. "And I had a couple of Mexican guys in there working for days to strip the old paint off."

"What's beadboard?" I asked. "Why'd it take so long?"

"It's about eight inches wide and has an extra groove in it, like this," he says while he draws an explanatory diagram on a board. "You have a real job to get the old paint out of that groove, and we struggled with it for days. Then one day I saw this bottle opener on my dash, the kind with a triangular end." He forms three of his fingers into the proper shape. "And I just thought about it. I mean, you could machine files to fit, but that's something I have neither the patience nor the skill to do. So I just took a file and brought that opener to a point, and we had a perfect tool to do the job. It didn't look like much of stripper, but we got that job done quick after that."

When I said I was doing "anthropological fieldwork" in Fredericksburg, Abel told me a story about a time when he had been younger and walking a freshly plowed field on his family's ranch in the country north of town.

"After a good rain you find a lot of arrowheads around here. One of my grandmother's uncles, my great-great-granduncle, if there is such a word, was captured by the Comanches and held prisoner for a while. He wrote a book about it," Abel said. (*Nine Years among the Indians* by George Lehmann. A. G. Greene's *The Last Captive* is a contemporary retelling of this story, a telling that, according to Abel, some of Lehmann's descendants think is inaccurate.) "He wrote about camping out with them on House Mountain, that's a place in southern Llano County that you can see from our ranch; it's a flat-topped mesa that looks like a house with a flat roof. Anyway, I was walking across this field when I turned up a stone blade, a small one like for a child to use, and I picked it up and in front of me was this mountain my uncle had written about, and that wasn't so long ago, maybe eighty years or so—I knew the man—and it just gave me, yeah, it just made me shiver," he said.

Abel paid me to help him with the ceiling in the old building. The work had been going more slowly than he planned because three heifers on his family's ranch were pregnant and every day for more than a week he had been driving out to check on them, particularly one that he thought might have trouble birthing. After we stopped for the day, Abel sat in his pickup, wrote me a check, and told me about what had occurred with the cattle.

"I had a great Mother's Day," Abel said. I thought the sarcasm in his voice stemmed from the memory of his mother's recent death, which he had told me about earlier, and the irony of a Mother's Day without a mother. But Abel went on to tell me about what he had discovered at the ranch when he'd gone out to check on the cattle: "I've never had to take a calf out in pieces before."

"I was looking for the one I thought was going to have trouble birthing, but she came toward me with a little calf running behind her. She came with her calf and so did another one, but the third one was laying with her head pressed up against the water tank. She was laying there, and her calf was still inside her. There was a tongue and one hoof sticking out of her, but that was it."

"Was it a breech birth?" I asked.

"No, she was presenting in the right position, but it was just such a huge calf. She couldn't get it out, and it was stuck in there. So I started to pull, trying to get it out. When I first started, that calf was still alive a little. I could feel its tongue was warm and wet, but I couldn't get it out. It just didn't want to budge, so I called the vet, and he told me to try to get her up and bring her in."

"I thought vets were supposed to come to the sick animal, not the other way around," I said. "They're getting as bad as doctors who won't make house calls."

"Well, I couldn't get her up, so I tied a rope to the calf's leg and pulled like hell, and managed to get it out to its hips, but then it got what they call 'hiplock,' and just wouldn't come any further. By this time the calf was dead. I called the vet again, and he said he'd come out. He cut the calf's body off as close to the cow as he could, and then we pushed the hindquarters back inside."

"To turn it around, so it would come out in a different direction?" I asked.

"Well, he took a piece of what they call 'piano wire'—it's not really piano wire, but more like a strong, braided wire—and reached up inside her to put it between the legs, then pulled it out while holding on to both ends. To cut the hindquarters apart. I reached in and pulled one, and it came out easy. The other one shot out right behind it."

"What about the heifer? Did she die?"

"She's still there, laying there, and I'm bringing hay and water to her to help her heal. She got up from where she was first laying and walked about twenty-five yards away, but couldn't go any further. The place where she's laying doesn't have any shade, but fortunately it's not the middle of a hot July."

"So the days are cool enough yet that she won't die from the heat? What about predators? Are there any animals, like coyotes, around here anymore that might try to take her?"

"There never used to be coyotes in that country at all. I mean you sometimes heard about somebody shooting one down around Luckenbach, but that's thirty miles away. I've never seen them, though I've heard them out there a few times."

"That seems strange to me, because I grew up in Nebraska, where my mom's from," I said. "Out there in the country you hear them howling all the time, and you can see them pretty often, too."

"Once every few years I hear them—not howling really, but yapping as they move back and forth beyond the fence around the lower field. But I don't think they'd try to take a full-grown heifer—a calf maybe, but a heifer's too big.

"There's bobcats too. But they're too small to bother a cow. One of my hunters told me that he saw a big bobcat once out near Puht Mountain. He said it was yellow and had a long tail, and that he thought it wasn't a bobcat, but a mountain lion. So there might be a few of them up there as well. Especially on Puht Mountain."

"What's that, Puht . . . ?"

"Puht Mountain, well it's also called Putman Mountain. I didn't even know it had another name until I moved into town. We always called it Puht. It's a steep-sided mesa with a flat top. There's a little hill beside it that we always called Haines Berg—*berg* is German for 'mountain'—and we always called it that because the Haineses used to own it. I looked on a map once, I don't remember if it was a county map or what . . ."

"Maybe it was a geological survey map?" I suggested, since I'd been looking at these kinds of maps for the area only a few days earlier.

"Maybe a survey map. The official name of Haines Berg—what we always called Haines Berg—is 'Lover's Rock.' I've asked around and nobody who's ever lived out there has ever called it that as far as I can tell. Nobody ever goes up there, onto Puht Mountain, so there could be all kinds of wildlife up there, and nobody would know it. Once I was down by the field when I saw this group of big sheep—they had long, thick horns that curled up a little at the back, but not all the way around into a spiral like a ram's. They were some species of Iranian sheep. Nobody I talked to had ever seen any of them before, and here were fifteen of them running wild. A pair of them must have escaped from one of the exotic game preserves around here, and they'd been up there on Puht Mountain long enough to make that big a herd, and nobody had ever seen them."

3. Ruby

> The distinctiveness of the Germans [as farmers in Texas] rested largely on a number of traits . . . these included greater intensity, productivity, and locational stability of the German farmers, as well as their higher rate of landownership. . . . the more intimate attachment to the land, which was manifested in the greater locational stability and avoidance of tenancy, was associated with the fact that the German put more into the land in the form of labor and capital and got more from it in terms of produce. . . . only in retrospect, as a citizen of an over-populated world, in which an ever-higher value is placed on the soil which nourishes man, can one view the Germans as superior farmers.
>
> Terry G. Jordan, *German Seed in Texas Soil: Immigrant Farmers in Nineteenth-Century Texas*

For the last year I've worked, more or less regularly, at Tante's Haus & Garten, an organic farm and country store. The jobs I am doing this year—hoeing, weeding, planting, repotting—were last year done by a middle-aged Mexican man who slipped away with his accumulated pay in the middle of winter. He said he had a family emergency to attend to. A month later he called from a border town, broke and asking for money to get his car fixed so he could come back. Ruby's husband, Dan, wouldn't send money, but he sent a friend to tow the man home. He came back drunk enough that he had to sleep for two days before he could talk straight. He disappeared again, this time for good, after Dan told him he had to sober up and work if he wanted to stay.

Ruby and Dan have been tending with care this piece of land ten miles outside of Fredericksburg for the past six years. In the midst of a primarily touristic economy, Ruby and Dan seem to be throwbacks to the careful farming methods Terry Jordan argues were the trademark of early German-Texas farmers. The land was owned by her great-aunt and great-uncle, and Ruby, whose name then was Simmonds, grew up nearby in her parents' house. After living on the Texas coast, Ruby returned to renew her connection to the place where she grew up.

The farm is actually quite small—the produce field is less than an acre, with about six acres of alfalfa hay grown each year to be used by Ruby's brother to feed horses. She returned to the place after twenty years away teaching home economics on the coast. Ruby says she returned because she wanted to get back to basics—a common enough desire in this time of longing. The difference between Ruby and Dan and most people who claim to seek a more basic life is that Ruby's return home is grounded in both a nostalgic ideal and a practical reality. Ruby commented about why she has chosen to grow food organically on the same piece of land that provided her ancestors with their subsistence: "People like my Tante knew how to take care of the land while they made a living from it. I wanted to see if I could learn how to do the same thing."

Personal experience underlies Ruby's decision to try to live sustainably. While she lived on the coast her husband worked for an aluminum plant that processes bauxite shipped in from other nations.

"My husband came home covered with red dirt from bauxite ore. It caked in his pores. He showered at work, and again when he got home, but his skin still left red streaks on the pillow in the mornings.

"There was one guy who fell off a bike into a puddle. They used bikes to get around the plant. It was a big place. My husband worked with a guy who was riding through a puddle, well I guess it wasn't too much more than a wet spot, but he fell off that bike and into that moisture and a week later he was dead. Whatever was in that puddle killed him. His skin started peeling and kept on peeling until his bones were showing in places, and then he just died. They didn't have any way to stop him from dissolving."

Such a lesson was not lost on Ruby. Her children lived in the same environment that killed that man. Her water came from ground saturated with those same chemicals. Not long after she and her husband divorced, she decided to return to the farmstead of her great-aunt and -uncle, who had both recently died. With her second husband, Dan, she has been renewing the ties to the place initiated by her forebears.

"When we moved back here, we just decided to do things the way my great-aunt and -uncle had always done them," Ruby says. "I know that they never used chemical fertilizers or pesticides, because they weren't available then. They always had a huge garden, and whenever I came to visit, Tante just piled me up with vegetables, and even sometimes canned goods."

Ruby's statement that she decided to do things just like her great-aunt and -uncle has both a bit of truth and a bit of nostalgia to it. It is true, indeed, that she uses no chemical inputs for her garden. But the economy of her small business—named Tante's Haus & Garten Country Store in honor of her great-aunt—resembles that of her ancestors in name alone.

First of all, Ruby's livelihood is not geared toward subsistence. Much of the family's own produce is grown on the farm, and the large flock of laying chickens provides eggs and occasional meat, but that is the extent to which the food grown is consumed "in haus." No staple crops such as wheat, rice, beans, or corn are grown in the garden—the parcel of land is too small for self-subsistence by most agricultural standards in this country.

In keeping with the region's status as a peach-producing area, they have a few small orchards, which they are successfully growing organically, despite statements by the local agricultural extension agent who claims peaches cannot be grown organically due to susceptibility to insect and disease damage.

Unlike her great-aunt and -uncle, Ruby and Dan use tractors to work the land. They have three small tractors—two old Fords and an ancient Farmall C. These are used primarily for plowing, cultivating between rows, and spreading compost in the field. In-row weeding is done by hand. They recently bought a huge new bucket loader for turning commercial-sized piles of compost.

In addition to selling produce and "whole food" groceries at the store, Ruby and Dan have begun a compost business in the last two years that is beginning to thrive. Tante's Haus compost is developing a regional reputation for being the best in the area. The reputation of this compost is not undeserved—it is a rich mixture of turkey waste from area commercial turkey farms, cedar mulch, cotton trash, and horse manure from area stables. People drive eighty miles one way from Austin, despite the availability of commercial compost from Austin companies, and the San Antonio International Airport uses tons of Tante's Haus compost each season in landscape maintenance.

Those Who Re-placed

1. John and Lois

There are as many intimate places as there are occasions when human beings truly connect. What are such places like? They are elusive and personal. They may be etched in the deep recesses of memory and yield intense satisfaction with each recall, but they are not recorded like snapshots in the family album, nor perceived as general symbols like fireplace, chair, bed, and living room that invite intricate explication. One can no more deliberately design such places than one can plan, with any guarantee of success, the occasions of genuine human exchange.

Yi-Fu Tuan, *Space and Place*

Regardless of the cause for wandering anywhere on planet Earth, I believe that every race is, in one way or another, trying to find the kitchen again, the hearth, a place to stop and prepare something to eat for spirit as well as body not only for themselves but for those called family. We are all searching for that place of belonging, of safety, of place; that locale where survival instincts and basic needs are fulfilled in a location that smells, yea verily, reeks of sanctuary because we hunger, figuratively and literally, for place.

Joyce Gibson Roach, *This Place of Memory: A Texas Perspective*

I should say that John and Lois are not like my family in any way. They are from the Northeast, university educated—he attended an experimental branch of Yale Art School during the Great Depression and she went to Bryn Mawr in the late forties/early fifties. He is a painter. She is a composer. They speak with an accent, but not one from any place I've ever visited.

I say all of this because, inexplicably, sitting with them in the sunny kitchen of their home to talk and eat lunch felt as homelike as the first time I sat down with Uncle Herbert and Aunt Barbara in their mobile home to eat bacon and eggs and drink coffee. The same tape player sat unobtrusively on the table among the plates and pickles. Lois bustled about laying out food and boiling water for tea much like Aunt Barbara had made coffee and eggs. We talked about some of the same things. It was a moment of some kind of recognition, though I don't know fully what that means. Lois is sixty-five, and John is seventy-eight. I am twenty-six. We are a half century apart in age.

John and Lois moved to Fredericksburg in 1970 to get away from the hectic life of New York, where John was then working as a commercial artist. Their move took place in the context of race riots, urban upheaval, and the "white flight" from cities which took place during the late sixties and into the seventies. Before we ate lunch, John and I sat in his studio for a few minutes, and he told me that he woke up shaking one night in New York. He was suddenly feeling the tensions of the place where he lived, and the pressures of the way he lived and worked in that place. He was working as a commercial artist, and he looked at his peer group and saw men in their thirties and forties dying from heart attacks. That is when John and Lois decided to move away from the hub of the U.S. art world to what was then considered the "artless" world of Texas.

Inside, over lunch, the three of us discussed their decision to move.

"We had seen a Rockefeller report that identified the Hill Country as a good place to live," John said.

"So it was a Rockefeller report that said this was the place to be for the healthiest climate?" I asked.

"Yeah. If anybody had said . . . now, we're talking about the sixties

John McClusky (1914–1994), born in New Haven, Connecticut, painted the people and places of the Hill Country for the last twenty-five years of his life. We met about a year before he died and spent many hours talking about the role of art and writing for conveying the power of place and what John called "the creative spirit." In John's mind, seeing your own community, understanding its history and the stories of the people who made it, and observing the lives of those who constantly re-define that community was an important enough theme to be the subject of an entire life's work.

I knew him for less than a year, but we planned to do a show together combining his images with my writings. The presentation here is not as it would have been had we created it together. It is a fragment of the stories we would have told together. I miss him deeply.

Photographs of the paintings are by Frank Minogue.

No place is a place until things that have happened in it are remembered as history, ballads, yarns, legends, or monuments.—Wallace Stegner, "The Sense of Place"

When we first moved to Fredericksburg in 1970 it was an old German community that still had many of the characteristics that defined it a hundred years ago. The landscape, too, still looked wild—the sky huge and overwhelming. It was very quiet. Quiet and wild at the same time.—John McClusky

When we moved to town everybody had a garden. Gradually many gardens have disappeared. Today most people in town get their food from stores, but this old gentleman still grows a beautiful garden. He gives most of what he grows to neighbors and the food bank.—John McClusky

There is something absolutely right about a big country wedding—outside, under a huge Texas sky, even the trees seem to be guests at the feast. This is a self-portrait, too. I'm the one bending over for a beer from the cooler.—John McClusky

A bakery can be the heart of a community. Simple sweets and breads, but talk around the tables revolves around the things that make a town work as a community—shared stories, concerns, and the joy of meeting together with neighbors and friends.—John McClusky

Why paint a ruined, abandoned, unused building? A painting of this nature becomes more than merely a recording of this house on a particular street in a particular place. It becomes a statement of awareness which, if the painting is forcefully enough done, will produce an emotional reaction upon the spectator that will expand his or her own experience.—John McClusky

When a community loses its memory, its members no longer know one another. How can they know one another when they have forgotten or never learned one another's stories? If they do not know one another's stories, how can they know whether or not to trust one another? People who do not trust one another do not help one another, and moreover they fear one another. And this is our predicament now. Because of a general distrust and suspicion, we lose one another's help and companionship.
—Wendell Berry, "The Work of Local Culture"

and I've indicated to you something of what the upheaval was at that time. As a matter of fact, my peer group was scattering. They were beginning to move out. They were beginning to move out because they couldn't survive in New York. And the first thought that comes to mind, of course, was, where can we live more economically? And yet carry on the work that we're trying to do? So we were looking for a place that was . . . healthwise certainly an important factor. We had two children at the time, and we were thinking about the factor, certainly, the educational factor. And that's what scared me, when we looked at the [Fredericksburg] schools back in 1970, they were a disaster."

"They were?" I asked.

"Yeah. It was August, oh maybe 104 degrees. No fans. No air conditioning. Ah . . . we were talking to the pastors. I'll give you a tip off, pastors are better to talk to than the chamber of commerce if you really want to know about a community! And what we saw really is that, in spite of many of the shortcomings that were in evidence when we looked at the community, there were some people here that really had no concern other than doing a fine job. And, you know, that's a wonderful thing; to celebrate that, that's primarily one of my purposes."

"You mean in your painting, and in your teaching—in your life's work?" I asked.

"Yeah, sure, and to emulate that, in the sense that I want to live a life that does the same thing, a life in which my concern is to celebrate the strengths and fineness of the place. But if anybody had said in 1969, in say, May of 1969 . . . May 1970, that we were going to live in Fredericksburg, Texas, we would've thought they were absolutely, totally insane. We were thinking . . . the islands off of Spain, many painters have gone there. So we started to make some inquiries, and I thought, what about the children? And we thought of the islands off the coast, the East Coast. And then we began to look at, again, the situation for the children, the cost factors. I mean, we could buy all the wine and liquors that you want for practically nothing, but to put a basement under a house would cost you more than a whole house would in some other portions of the world, you know. Everything had to be shipped in. And my brother was moved down [to Texas], during the Second World War. And he kept saying, 'Why don't you take a look at Texas. It's growing, it's exploding.' And he was thinking primarily of Dallas and Houston. And I had never given it much thought because, basically, at that time Texas hardly existed in the art world. It doesn't now, really. It's even now considered provincial. We haven't gotten much over the first step. In this case they're very chauvinistic, to say the least. But I went, and I did exactly what I tell my students they should never do. I took a collection of paintings in a folio. Now you don't do that, and hit a city and go from door to door with them, it's . . . it's ridiculous."

"Why is that ridiculous?"

"Well, it gets you into an absurd position of hawking your work. . . . Who wants to bother with you?"

"Yeah, I guess it's like you're selling vacuum cleaners or something."

"Yeah, sure. And you put yourself in a terrible position. But I got on a plane, came down to Dallas and I took a look at the Sunday paper at the list of galleries, you know, in the arts section. Started at the top and just went on through. And some of them I didn't even go in, I knew they were not for me. There were several that were interested. And I chose one. But then, what are you going to do? You can't serve a Dallas gallery from New England. So, we were almost compelled, then, to make the move," he said and chuckled softly. "And, of course, being Yankees, and conscious of space and distance from that particular narrow point of view, when we came here we were just absolutely confounded by the enormity of nothingness! And if you've been a Yankee all your life, and you're a painter, see, how do you paint this?" He gestures as if to the hills and sky surrounding town.

"You know, it's really quite an experience. Well, we heard about the Hill Country . . . we did the whole state. Finally we settled here. And the night before we did, we ended up in Kerrville . . . not the night before we settled here, but before we chanced upon Fredericksburg. And we had been traveling all day. It was August. It was extraordinarily hot. We had a great big Oldsmobile. No air conditioning. And Katy was only four, and Lois would hold Katy, then I would hold Katy, and we'd be absolutely soaked.

"We held her when she slept, napped." Lois explained.

"And we hit Kerrville on this particular night, and there was something—a convention of some kind—taking place. And we couldn't find a motel. And we looked and looked and looked."

"We also had a cat," Lois added.

"And it was getting later and later and later. And finally we found one way in the back somewhere. And the room, well it was terrible—cockroach in the bed, and smelled so badly. Oh, we were hungry and the children were very, very tired, and we asked for a restaurant. There was a place called The Greasy Spoon, and if ever there was a place that was named accurately . . . it was absolutely horrible! And Lo and I sat there that night, and we said, 'My God! What have we done?' We had a lovely home, we had a group of friends up there. Here we are in the middle of nowhere and . . ."

"You had already sold your home?"

"Oh yeah, sure. As a matter of fact, part of . . . we had arranged it so that when the sale was completed, they would permit us to rent it for storage for one month. And in that month's time we were to find a place down here to live. Well, we made it, but—"

"'Where angels fear to tread . . . ,'" Lois added.

"And we came to Fredericksburg, and it was clean and neat and we were immediately impressed and our spirits just rose. We thought we'd stop and talk to a realtor, just for kicks. Astonished at the prices, compared to the North. We decided we better take a look at the rest of the state, and we did. And finally decided to come back here. The fact that this is a higher elevation makes a big difference. The difference between here and San Antonio is noticeable. We have Katy who lives there, a teacher, our daughter. She loves to come to Fredericksburg."

"So when you drove up that main street of Fredericksburg that first time, how different was it from what it's like now? Can you remember?"

"It's just more developed now," Lois said. "I think at that time, maybe, at least half the buildings on Main Street were empty."

"They were empty?"

"And maybe not in that great a shape," she said. "But in the meantime, during the late seventies, early eighties, so many people moved in from places like Houston and Dallas, and they were trying to invest right off. They would buy land, so that they could write it off—'Didn't make any money on that ranch,' you know, for taxes. And a lot of people moved in and bought up these old buildings, and finished them, and re-did them, and the town now, the buildings you know, well, they're in great shape because of money moving in."

"It was really a depressed area," John said. "Most of the stores were empty. As a matter of fact, we were quite convinced . . . we looked at the

White Elephant and that drugstore alongside it, and there was a dental lab there, and then the clinic, and there's a home where the original family still lives. And we thought that was a put-on . . . Yeah, well, that whole collection of buildings there from the White Elephant on down. And they own that building in back that stood empty, has stood empty all through these years. Slowly decaying."

"So you thought it was a 'put-on'? What do you mean, like they had—"

"Looked like a movie set, yeah. What in the world is the White Elephant? Now obviously, not a badly done building, but obviously at the same time obviously . . . well, you can understand, we were in Texas, thoughts come to your mind. Was it just some crazy man or something—he came from Africa? The guy who had it built just liked elephants, and they actually [chuckles] formed the shape and poured it and stuck it up there. Now if you look at that building, it's beautifully done. Oh my. You're talking about a great deal of skill in some of these structures that shows a lot of loving attention that we couldn't afford to give today. You'd either do it mechanically, or you wouldn't do it."

2. *Alicia*

In most respects the Heartland story could serve as a paradigm of rural conservation efforts around the country. Like people in rural Maine or southern Appalachia, the residents of Stonewall and Comfort and Sisterdale are struggling to preserve the work of local culture without throwing up fences or treating the Heartland as a rural museum. Fences never make good neighbors, and they don't work anyway. Change is coming. The challenge for the Heartland Council is to steer it in the right direction, away from blind exploitation.

David Dillon, "Deep in the Heart," in *Historic Preservation*

The theory is that the more folks know about the region the more likely they'll want to preserve it. . . . "It's not heritage in a box," says [the Heartland council director]. . . . "It's a tapestry. And [the council] is a way to make that richness more appreciated, understood and accessible."

Michele Stanush, "Hill Country Treasures," in *Austin American-Statesman*, June 6, 1993

It is not easy for me to write about Alicia. I suppose every life has its share of misunderstandings and missed connections. My relationship with Alicia, which began full of promise for mutually beneficial work, ended in silence and disappointment. Alicia moved to the Hill Country from San Antonio, and is the director of a nonprofit organization, The Texas Heartland Council, which works to preserve the character of the Hill Country. In her own words, it is an organization trying to "manage change" constructively to keep the richness and vitality of the region alive while it undergoes huge shifts in its economic and social structure.

What is the Heartland Council?

The obvious place to begin is with the self-description included in the Council's mission statement:

> The LBJ Heartland Council is a 501(c)3 non-profit organization, incorporated in the fall of 1988. Its mission is to conserve the natural and cultural resources of the area in ways that accommodate change and create opportunities for the region's citizens. Towards that end, the Council develops programs and services to
>
> • instill an environmental ethic through public outreach and education
> • foster regional coordination and cooperation
> • stimulate economic diversity

But this is organizational rhetoric that, while reflecting self-consciously constructed definitions, does little to evoke the human relations to place and people that comprise the Council.

I became embroiled in the work of the Council in a rather off-hand manner. I was working at Tante's Haus & Garten, doing field work, pulling weeds, planting potatoes. I repotted plants. This was digging in the dirt and getting my fingers filthy with soil and compost. I loved it.

One day, while I was picking tomatoes ripening in the late summer sun, Alicia introduced herself to me as the director of the Heartland Council. We couldn't shake hands—I was sweaty and my fingers were green from the tomatoes—but we talked for a while, and she told me about what the Council was doing. I'll admit that I don't remember exactly what she said, but it was enough to suggest to me that all the writing about "place" I'd been doing in the past year was related to her project. We parted with promises of further conversations and I finished gathering fruit.

Somewhere in the whirlwind of a busy harvest season, and a course-altering shift in my life—Mitra, my partner for the past two years, called with news that we were going to be parents—I never got back to talking with Alicia. Suddenly my life seemed to swing wildly onto a different course. I flew to Portland, Oregon, where Mitra was doing her fieldwork, and we agreed we would return together to Central Texas to have our child.

I had to get a full-time job. First I dove earnestly into working for a custom cabinetmaker in Fredericksburg. I loved the smell of freshly sawn boards, the way my fingers skated over the smooth sanded surface of cabinets. But this was not a place truly focused on making cabinets; it was a business interested in making money, with cabinets as the vehicle. A week of high-pressure, "get-the-things-made" attitude surrounded by the din and thunder of power saws and electric compressors convinced me I needed to seek other work.

That's when the Heartland Council entered my life again. Alicia called, explaining that she wanted to talk to me about a job. She was looking for someone to take a part-time position with the Council. They needed someone to take on a number of roles that eventually became defined over the six months I worked there as "communications coordinator" and "social science intern."

Working for the Council seemed not only like a good way to continue thinking about what place means in a contemporary setting, but also a way to contribute some of the skills I'd been working on for so many years—especially listening to stories and writing—to the community where I lived. After my first week at work, I wrote in my notebook:

> Talking w/ M. last night—she said she'd never be able to do this
> kind of work—it's too "officey," and perhaps too uncritically "activist."
> I commented that if I'm trying to understand the way "places" get
> understood, created, changed in the contemporary world, then it's
> important to understand the roles of institutions and organizations,
> both within the region and beyond. Such institutions and organiza-
> tions are not just peripheral to the social construction of places, they
> are integral to modern/postmodern life.

Alicia and I spent many days working together in a cold room in the Old Blanco County Courthouse that served as the Council's headquarters. The Courthouse had been saved through the efforts of the Blanco community from being carried off by a landowner who wanted to move it to his ranch and use it as a house. This event is described by David Dillon:

> Precisely because it is a grassroots organization, involving people from throughout Blanco, Hays, and Gillespie counties, the Council sometimes succeeds where official bureaucracies would have failed. Its first coup was helping the local historical society raise $250,000 to buy back the Blanco County Courthouse from a developer who wanted to dismantle and move it stone by stone to his ranch in East Texas. (Dillon 1993)

My primary role was to work closely with Alicia to draw together several of the projects the Heartland Council had been working on for the past year. This primarily took the form of writing grant proposals to various agencies to find funding for the next step in the Council's development. As a grassroots activist working with people and groups throughout the region, Alicia juggled many different voices and ideas about what the region should look like and how it should be preserved. One of her favorite metaphors for the work we were doing was that of a tapestry or weaving. After we'd worked together for about three months, I wrote:

> Jan. 4: Spent the day pulling together various strands written over the past few months into a "notebook" for planning over the next five years & to use as basis for organizing the spring/summer series "Learning the Language of Place." Alicia thinks like a weaver—she actually made one large weaving that was a conglomeration of materials added one after another to the piece. Her boss at LAL [Learning about Learning, an experimental school that operated in San Antonio] used the weaving to show the way Alicia thinks. The boss would bring people in to show them the huge weaving, and she would mock whisper, "That's precisely the way she thinks!" I pointed out that that metaphor of weaving was apt—we've been spinning yarn for the past three months, with each of the components we've been writing as a different kind of fiber finished and set aside to be worked into the

whole tapestry later. This frustrated me for a while b/c I kept wanting to mail each thing out as we got it into some kind of coherent draft so it would become something discussed and used in a larger context. Realize now that sending those things out would have been premature, b/c people would have had trouble making heads or tails of the stuff without the vision/context. Now we are getting it all together, and it feels substantial and promising.

That promise went on to become a series of workshops, tours, special events, and exhibits revolving around the natural and human history of the region. There were picnics on the river where local oral historian Carroll Smith told stories and gourmet cooks made meals using only local produce, tours of geologic features, car trips around watersheds, visits to innovative farms and orchards, and an all-day, kickoff event held at the 6,000-acre ranch of a conservation-minded Council benefactor.

But somewhere along the way, my relationship with Alicia soured. In February we went to San Francisco together to attend a week-long workshop on exhibit development held by The Exploratorium, an award-winning "hands-on" museum of science. I felt lost in that workshop, wondering what exactly I was supposed to do with the experience there. In retrospect I see that our working relationship fell apart, primarily because we did not clearly define what my role was supposed to be. This was in part due to Alicia's organizing style, which was to leave things ambiguous enough at first so that individuals and organizations would volunteer to take on certain projects. I did not, however, rise to the task of imagining how to design exhibits around the natural and human resources of our home region. I couldn't get my mind around the idea that this was an adequate way to "preserve" the landscapes and places of the Hill Country.

As spring began, and the date for the "kickoff" event approached, Alicia and I began to have a more difficult time working together. I felt hollow as the work progressed, less connected to it. Alicia, feeling the pressure to "get it all together" in time, became dissatisfied with an apparent reticence on my part. We had several clashes that I think left us both frustrated and a little confused about what had happened. My reticence was equally the result of questioning the potential success of these self-conscious methods to revitalize place through tourism on the one hand, and the impending birth of my daughter on the other. Alicia and

I agreed that I would stay on with the Heartland Council through the beginning of the program series, then I would withdraw as a part-time employee.

In one of the small ironies that sometimes creep into life, my daughter was born at noon on exactly the day that the kickoff celebration took place. Instead of getting into my truck and rattling out to the ranch to watch the metaphoric "birth" of the "Learning the Language of Place" series, I stayed at home to participate in the midwife-assisted delivery of my daughter, Selene.

Except for an "art/idea" exhibit I put together using the paintings of John McClusky, I did not work for the Council after Selene's birth. I went on to put together jobs waiting tables and working on a nearby ranch, and Alicia found another person to take on the roles I had been performing for the Heartland Council. Alicia continued her efforts to define the tourist economics of the place, while my own work life took another path.

3. Alessandro, then Marion

> The trouble lay in the land itself. The soil, as it turned out, was surprisingly thin, the stone outcrops everywhere, the rainfall precarious. . . . The land was not only untillable where it was visibly hilly, but it was also hilly where it appeared to be flat. Grass "as high as stirrups" waved in the wind with pleasing symmetry that made the landscape look level, but when the grass was burned and cleared for plowing, the "pasture" too had often vanished. The land was maddeningly uneven, not every ten yards or so, but every yard, sometimes every foot. And when the rains came, the water cut along the unevenness, washing the inch-deep soil away, revealing a field suddenly strewn with rocks. The grass had concealed some frightening truths. In all but bottomland pastures where topsoil had accumulated over hundreds of years, the grass should never have been plowed.
>
> Lawrence Goodwyn, *Coming to Terms:*
> *The German Hill Country of Texas*

He's a little guy, Alessandro is, but strong.

In addition to working as a waiter at a local restaurant, I work a couple days a week for a woman, Marion, who's got sixty acres near Hye.

Lately I've been taking Alessandro with me to help with the work. We're working on stopping soil erosion and repairing the damage done by the land's previous owner, who ran horses on this hillside that was marginal grazing ground to begin with, and is now in a serious state of degradation. Mostly the work consists of spreading rotting hay and straw bales, thousands of them, on bare spots—mulching on an acre-wide scale. It became clear both to Marion and me that I needed help hauling and spreading the bales, so I asked José and Alessandro, the busboys at the Mesa Cafe, whether they'd like to make some extra money. José worked once, then sent his more fit and much younger nephew to help the next time.

I like Alessandro. He's enthusiastic about work, any kind. Throws himself into it smiling. He speaks a little English. I speak a little Spanish. We carry on conversations in a halting hybrid language. He tells me about the ranch his family owns in Mexico, a place in the foothills of some mountains north of Mexico City. This fall has been Alessandro's second season in Texas. He and José plan to go back after New Year's and stay for a few months to help with the bigger chores on the ranch—branding, butchering, and such. Then they'll return here to bus tables.

"We got a good place there," Alessandro says while we drive twenty miles out to Hye in the morning. "But there's no way to make money there. We eat good, got a good house we're making, but no money."

During the seasons here, Alessandro lives with his uncle José, José's wife, and a variable number of other relatives in a two-bedroom trailer house on the edge of Fredericksburg. "It looks like here," Alessandro says, speaking of his home in Mexico, "but has higher hills; then come mountains."

"Do you have a lot of friends there? Do they miss you when you're gone?"

"Most my friends do like I do and work somewhere else some of the year to make money. Come home when they can."

"How about girlfriends?"

"All the girls like me," he says and flashes a smile that makes you believe it. "I'm not in a hurry to get married."

When we get to Marion's place, Wilory Farm, I ask Alessandro to push the button for the gate. We drive down the slope on the gravel road Marion had built around her sixty acres. It looks like a big looping racetrack surrounding infields of slowly expanding stands of native grasses, ryegrass and clover. Marion's been seeding this place heavily the past two years with strips of long-stemmed grasses and nitrogen-fixing legumes. The ryegrass grows quickly, filling in until the longer-cycle perennial grasses get a chance to grab hold. It still looks like a place that has been overgrazed, with lots of rock and bare dirt showing where water from heavy rains runs off, but beginnings of green promise more to come.

I park on the road, and we walk over to the pile of moldy hay and straw bales dumped near some of the biggest bare spots. Marion has the guys at the feed store in Johnson City keep their ears open for people who have spoiled hay in their barns or fields. She buys the stuff cheap and that's her primary weapon against soil erosion. It's slow, but inexpensive, and as I'm discovering over the months I've been working for her, amazingly effective. We work, mostly in silence, all day. Breaking bales, spreading, sweating. Occasionally we stop to admire the way a circling turkey vulture floats on the updrafts in the clear blue sky. Alessandro spreads his arms, and his small body looks like it might lift into the air, too.

Marion has got a story to tell!

I tend to think of her as something of a "latter-day techno-monk." She lives alone, and her life is simple, but rich in activity and thought. I also think of her as "the goat woman" because she has a herd of about twenty goats that she uses primarily as range improvement tools. They browse the shrubby juniper that springs up and robs the grasses of nutrients and moisture. She feeds them amaranth and other hard-seeded grains, some of which even a goat's stomach can't digest. When the grains have passed through and been dropped onto the ground, they're contained in a perfect pellet of moisture and fertilizer—it's her indirect way of seeding for the future health of her land. We feed out bales of fresh alfalfa over the bare spots near her house, and the goats deposit their droppings in the places most in need of it.

That kind of thoughtful and efficient "technology" is typical of the way Marion's mind works. She used to be a computer programmer in the early days of the computer boom (late sixties/early seventies). It was a time when computer capacities tended to be more limited, so programming tended to be tighter than today. Programs were designed to do things as efficiently as possible, with little waste. She's still an avid computer-game aficionado, but she complains about the sloppiness of a lot of recent programming.

"There's not much carefulness in many new games," she says. "They do a lot of neat things, but take up way too much memory, and tend to be slower than they have to be."

Marion's made herself a tidy place. She designed her own small house and hired some local builders to put it up. It's made of cinderblock, painted cool white to reflect the intense Texas sun. A single, interior room is divided by bookshelves into a sleeping area, a computer work area, a kitchen, and an area for just sitting and working out compositions on her guitar. In addition to being a soil conservationist, Marion's a classical guitarist and composer.

She used to be a dairy-goat and nut farmer along the Rio Grande River. As a single woman and a farmer, she did not exactly fit the female stereotypes of the area, and many of the people she had contact with took a while to get used to her.

"Mexican men who came to look at my goats would always ask where my husband was," she told me one day while we headed out to the milkroom to feed the goats and milk Lucille, the one lactating goat Marion currently has for her own milk use. "Since I never had one to drag out, they'd finally give up and talk to me."

She lets the "special goats"—Lucille's two kids; Prisca, an old and especially loved goat; and three other adults who get supplements and attention each day—into the paddock outside the building. She pours feed pellets into two troughs for the remaining goats, then lets her inner circle into the milkroom, where they go to their appropriate places and push their heads through stanchion openings. She locks each one in place, and they nose down into their respective feed buckets and munch on their organic oats, almonds, and other goodies. These goats eat high on the hog.

Lucille hops up on the milking stand and puts her head through the stanchion where Marion pours in her rations. Marion begins milking, and I head out to work on the mulching.

One morning, Mitra and I load Selene up in my pickup and drive out to Wilory Farm together. It's the first time Mitra has been here, though she and Marion have become friends during Marion's trips into town. We are heading to Marion's for a little ritual. We're going to plant a tree, a chinquapin oak, which Marion says is resistant to the oak wilt that is wiping out entire stands of live oak trees in the Hill Country.

Marion comes out to greet us.

"I've got a good place picked out for the Selene tree," she says. She's wearing her canvas hat, the same one she always wears when she works in the heat. It has several large safety pins fastened on the crown, because Marion says she's learned during her years of ranch life that they come in handy when you least expect it. For example, you can use safety pins to hold torn cloth together when you accidentally snag yourself on barbed wire.

Marion grabs a spade from the toolshed, Mitra brings Selene wrapped in a blanket against the sun, and I carry a bucket containing the six-foot-tall tree and its rootball. We walk through a gate and up the hill about fifty yards from the house, where Marion tells me to make the hole. We're in the middle of a grassy savanna spotted with other trees that Marion has planted here. This is her future "grove," and this oak will have an honored spot in it. I begin digging and find that the soil here is thicker and blacker than on most of the rest of the ranch. The previous owner didn't run his horses here as often I guess. I make the hole deep enough to bury the rootball's crown, and four or five times wider than the ball.

Marion drags a hose out from the toolshed, and we begin our ritual attempt to root Selene in this place. Before we lower the tree into the hole, Mitra drops in the placenta and afterbirth we have been saving in a freezer container until we could arrange a day to do this. As we take turns shoveling the backfill in, we mix in some Tante's Haus compost, and a few other soil supplements. After the hole is full, Marion uses the hose to soak the soil around the oak. The blood and tissue that nurtured Selene before she was born will become part of the soil that feeds this tree. In metaphor at least, she will always have roots in this place.

Midnights at the Mesa Cafe

1. Liar's Poker

We've been closed for an hour, and they're well into a long game of liar's poker. Each of them long ago passed the one-drink courtesy tip that Randy, the owner, gives each of his employees after they work a shift.

Cierto's sucking down the dregs of his second Long Island Iced Tea, as well as nursing a beer. Mike, who is the manager, Roberto, Tory, and Ken are all drinking various kinds of beer, and José and Alessandro, the two Mexican busboys, are sitting in a booth nearby drinking frosted mugs of Shiner Bock. Ketch, the cook who's still in high school, is stuck drinking a soda, I think because Randy got busted once for allowing a minor to drink. Jake, the other male waiter besides me and Roberto, isn't here. A few nights ago, one of the cooks caught him kissing another guy in the parking lot out back. So many people gave him so much shit about being a "fucking fag" that Jake went home and slashed his wrists, so tonight he's recovering in the state hospital in Kerrville.

Pepper, who usually doesn't stay for a drink, is sitting with me at a table by the fireplace and we're talking about Jake. "He ought to just move out of this stupid town," she says. "He should move to a city somewhere and be whatever he needs to be. People are too small-minded here."

This is the third time she's said this, so I simply nod and agree. She just wants somebody to whom she can vent.

Roberto seems to be ahead in the game; he's got lots of dollar bills piled in front of him. I don't quite follow the rules, something about comparing the serial numbers on the dollar bills you have in your pocket, but you bluff most of the time, claiming you've got five eights that will beat the last person's four sixes, and it keeps going round the circle, the claims getting bigger until somebody finally calls. Whoever has the highest hand that they *didn't* lie about, wins all the dollars in play for that round. Needless to say, given how confused I am by the whole thing, I don't play, but simply sit sipping beer, listening to Pepper, watching, talking, and looking around the cafe.

Picture this scene: an old stone building that has served as Civil War munitions factory, smithy, old-style German restaurant, and now plays the part of a southwestern-style cafe. There are mounted deer and elk heads on the walls, beer signs, a wooden bar backed by mirrors, high, dark recesses in the ceiling guarded by swirling ceiling fans. Up front a rolled-down curtain painted with advertisements hides a stage. The cafe's centerpiece is a large limestone fireplace topped by a wooden mantel and the mounted head of a huge longhorn bull. This is the Mesa Cafe, a restaurant named for the geologic formations that give the Hill

Country its character. It used to be called Oma's, but Randy Thompson changed the name when he bought the business a few years ago. Despite offering sausage, sauerkraut, and red cabbage on the menu, Randy decided to give it a southwestern twist to try and steer away from the German *gemutlichkeit* opportunism of the rest of the community. It's a strategy that seems to have worked, pulling in a certain type of customer, the "western-o-phile" ranchers, the hippie rock climbers, the town Episcopalians (Randy's family's church).

I worked at the Mesa as a waiter for about six months, making a living during the first half year of my daughter's new life, and learning about the way that people my age find an economic place in the tourist economy of Fredericksburg.

2. The Good, the Bad, and the Famous

Are we talking about the same Marlboro Man?

He and Romelia lived on this fabulous piece of real estate in the hill country, outside Fredericksburg. Beautiful house on a bluff, next to some cattle ranches. You'd think you were miles from civilization, deer and wild turkey and roadrunners and hawks and all that, but it was only a ten-minute drive to town. They had a big Fourth of July party there once and invited everybody who was anybody. Willie Nelson, Esteban Jordan, Augie Meyers, all that crowd.

Sandra Cisneros, *Woman Hollering Creek and Other Stories*

Okay, I'll admit, I don't know these people—Madeleine Stowe and Tommy Lee Jones—who they are, why they came here, what being in the Hill Country means to them. But I'll tell you this much, in the restaurant where I work I've either waited on them or seen them waited on, and they're re-placers, both of them. They have ranches in the region, and appear to consider these places parts of their "homes."

All the waitstaff and kitchen staff is buzzing on a Thursday night in October.

"Madeleine's here," Rikki, a Latina waitress, tells me as I fill a customer's iced tea glass at the urn in the wait station.

"Who?" I ask.

"Madeleine Stowe," she says. "You know, the actress. And her husband, the guy from HBO, is here too."

I have no idea who she's talking about, because I haven't seen a feature film in the theater since I walked out of some Robin Williams debacle three years ago. I'm tired from a long, stupid shift of plopping plates of cooked-from-scratch food in front of sunburned tourists.

Mike, the manager and bartender, comes into the kitchen and tells me I've got table A5 on the patio.

"You dog," Rikki says. "She tips good."

I go outside to wait on the couple at the table, mid-thirties, both of them attractive in a "regular" sort of way. She orders a bowl of the chicken-tortilla soup (a house specialty) and a burger. He orders a steak and some vegetables. They're friendly enough. Nothing out of the ordinary.

"What did she say?" Rikki asks when I bring the order back to the cooks. Cierto, the half-Indian, half-Hispanic cook is practically swooning into the french frier. "I got to see her," he says.

"She said, 'I'll take a bowl of soup and a burger,'" I answer. "Then she said, 'thank you.'"

"She's so cool," Rikki says and pushes out through the door into the dining room.

What does ordering soup and a burger have to do with cool? Cierto puts her burger and the guy's steak on to grill while I ladle up the soup and put tortilla strips on the plate around it. He slips out the back to see whether he can peek through the latticework onto the patio where she's sitting.

Later, Rikki lists some of the movies Ms. Stowe has been in: "*Last of the Mohicans, Bad Girls,*" but I haven't seen any of them. Then she says, "You know, her husband does that comedy series on HBO." And I still don't know anything.

This is not the first I've heard about "famous" folk moving into the area. Willie Nelson's been a fixture in the area for decades, and there was that whole Luckenbach, Texas, thing with Hondo Crouch for years. But there's a new wave on, too. One local realtor spread rumors that she had been showing various properties to Barbra Streisand. It's as if Fredericksburg boosters don't believe that this area qualifies as a *place* until somebody well known takes an interest in the region.

Here's my second story about restaurant run-ins with the rich and famous:

A Sunday afternoon, and the Mesa is pretty quiet, the lull that comes between the lunch rush and the evening supper crowd. Only two waits are still on duty right now: me and Jane, the older woman who is the de facto head waitress of the place. Jane gets a single customer at table number three, a booth hidden round the corner from the front door of the place. She goes over to get the customer's drink order. Mike and I are standing by the bar and we hear the man's voice and see that it is the actor Tommy Lee Jones. He orders iced tea and a bowl of soup, and Jane goes back to get it.

A customer stands at the bar waiting to pick up a drink, and she asks Mike if she can use the phone. He hands her the cordless unit, and she dials some numbers and suddenly she's breathlessly babbling into the phone, "Hi, it's me. I'm at the Mesa Cafe and you'll never guess who just walked in. It's Tommy Lee Jones! He's here, yeah. He's sitting in the corner and I'm looking right at him." Now this is looking and sounding like a stupid movie scene, isn't it? He hears the woman and is clearly agitated at being recognized. She goes on for a minute before Mike finally says, "Excuse me, ma'am, this is a business line," and she looks at Mike funny and shrugs and says good-bye and goes back to her table, forgetting her drink.

By this time, Jane has returned with Mr. Jones's order, but he's feeling put-out and surly, and he snaps at her, "I know what you people here are all about. You're just interested in snapping up money from the tourists. All this town is interested in is making money." And he eats his soup quickly, drinks his glass of tea, and leaves a few dollars on the table. Daylight floods into the dim room as he opens the door and stomps out.

What should I call this vignette? Shoot-out at the Mesa Corral starring Tommy Lee Jones?

3. Roberto Says

I ain't always been a plate slinger, you can believe that. Up until a few years ago I run a dozer, a big one, on all kinds of jobs from here to West Texas and back. And I knew how to do it right too, not that I want to brag, but people paid me good because they trusted that I could get the job done, quick and right.

My sister, the one who got hit crossing the street, she used to come with me all over the place and pick up work cooking for the crew. If I got a job over toward San Angelo, she'd tag along and make her money too. She came with me out to El Paso. Abilene. Midland. Wherever she could get work. That's how she ended up with three kids from three different men. Moving round's easier on a man—and I'm not saying that's how it should be, but that's the way it is.

That was all before the two accidents. Those two things that happened within two weeks of one another that changed my life and left me here, hustling tables for a living and drinking free beer after the place closes.

I'm not too old, but I'm still older than you might think looking at me in this green shirt. I been around long enough to know how things usually go for my family, so I'm not saying what happened to me was unusual or anything. My old man died working at a quarry just outside town. When he got the job, he knew what it was gonna be. The ad in the paper even said it. "Quarry hand wanted. Heavy lifting and willing to work under hazardous conditions required. Must work long hours under all weather conditions." He went out to the place and found out an old drinking buddy of his was foreman of the place, and he thought it was his lucky day.

And for a while it was. He worked in the hot sun all that summer and on through the rainy time in September, and he was pulling down more than enough money to keep all us kids in clothes and fed. My mother was able to work less in the laundry in town, and she got to spend more time looking after us kids. My father wasn't sloppy in his work; he took care to be clear whenever there was blasting going on, and he handled the crane and such real well—I guess it's a talent that runs in my family, working with heavy machinery. But somebody messed up. Seems like somebody always does, and my dad got his leg blown up, and bled to death before anybody could even call the ambulance or anything.

Mama went back to working full-time and then some, and not too much later I started doing whatever construction work I could get hired for at sixteen.

I'm not telling you this to make you feel sorry for me. You're one nice guy, and I just feel like talking tonight. Maybe I'm drunk. Maybe not. But talking feels good.

My sister's kids, they didn't have anybody but me and my mom then. And Mom takes good care of them, even now when two of them are teenage punks and the youngest one's headed that way too. It's too bad my sister didn't have any girls. At least they could get married then, and my mom wouldn't have to watch out for them anymore. She can hardly speak English and every couple a weeks she's down at the Gillespie courthouse, bailing one or another grandson out a trouble.

I guess maybe I'll have to stay living in my mom's garage, the apartment above it, for a long time. She needs my help, and besides, I can't afford a place of my own in this town anymore. Fucking tourists. Everything costs more now. Too many people want too much now. They want a house in San Antonio, and a Sunday house in this town too. Me, I'd settle for anything that was just mine, but who makes enough waiting tables to buy a house?

I won a lot of money tonight, maybe fifty bucks. Let's go get another beer at the Backdoor Bar. They got Shiner there too.

4. Tory, Lost in the Weeds

He's over there, somewhere, downstream in the dark. He wanted to show me something, but I think he's forgotten what it was, and now he's just wandering without purpose in the brush by the creek. I should go back a few steps, I guess, and explain how we ended up here on this moonlit, misty night.

Tory tends bar at the place where I'm a waiter. He's got nothing going for him but youth, which is passing fast, and a strong arm. I've never seen anybody put him down in arm wrestling, and I've seen some big guys try. He's just kind of a stringy looking guy, but he won't give up, and he says that's about 92 percent what it takes to win when you're arm wrestling. Not that it does him any good. They never wrestle for money. Nobody's dumb enough to do that, because they *know* Tory's not going to lose.

We've got this saying at the Mesa. Whenever somebody gets so busy, so slammed, that they can't keep up with what they're supposed to be doing for their job, we say that person is "in the weeds," and that's where Tory seems to be most of the time. Not only at work, which is understandable because we get really busy most nights, but *all* the time, like life just has too much going on for him to keep up.

That's not to suggest that I don't like Tory, because truth is, he's like a part of me; I mean, when I look at him coming down the street, looking real beat, it's like seeing some young version of myself. But Tory, he's got this way of looking that way all the time, like he'd just fold it all in and give away the dollar in a minute.

He tells me a lot of stories about this friend of his, Miley, who's living in a school bus or something on a commune in Vermont. Tory thinks this Miley's got it all going on, but it sounds to me like Miley's just kind of slacking there, sleeping in somebody else's bed and drinking water out of somebody else's tap. Tory says Miley's always talking about the Big Changes that are happening, but Miley sounds to me like he wouldn't know it if somebody changed his underwear for him. He sounds like a pompous ass.

But not Tory. Tory's better than his life seems to be letting him be. He's got a willingness to help a friend that you just don't see much anymore. He's the only person I know who shows up whenever you need a pile of stuff moved, or a heavy thing heaved over the fence. He's the only one who came to help me load the truck when Mitra and I packed up to move north.

Notes on a Return Trip Visit

It's been more than two years since I moved away from Fredericksburg. More than two years since I visited. And four years, more or less, since I started writing this sprawling pile of words.

The first night I got in I stayed at a motel. My plan for the trip was to stay with Lois, but she travels often since John died, and wouldn't arrive home until the next day. The guy at the motel hooked me with a story. I had been planning to go on to another, cheaper motel near the edge of town. I stopped to ask his price, and he told me a story about his great-grandfather, who he said had been a fife player under Robert E. Lee. After he told me the formal stuff about the man being a Confederate soldier and receiving a pension from the government, he told me about the time his great-grandfather had been coming home from playing fiddle at a party. He was drunk, and his wife didn't know it was him at the door, so she fired a rifle at him through the door. The bullet passed through his coat, but didn't hit him, and when he called out, his wife realized who he was. The family kept that coat as a relic. "So you just watch out where you play that thing," he said and pointed to my flute. "You never know when you might get shot at." "Well, maybe I just need to make sure I don't drink and play at the same time!" "Oh, drinking's all right," he said, "but watch out for somebody with a rifle pointed your way." I laughed and went out, but after walking a little ways, I decided the story was worth the extra five bucks and went back to register.

He gave me a room at the Schmidt Inn, which was a real motel-style building—single units with covered carports connecting them to the next room—that he assured me was the oldest continuously operating motel in town. "My wife's grandfather put up the first eight units back in the twenties. And it's been open ever since. The other motels in town, they've all had their bad times. The Sunday House was closed for a few years. The Peach House. All the others are either really new or have been closed off and on. My wife's father ran it after his dad retired. My wife was born in that stone house right there." He gestured across the street. "And now we run that place and this one too."

In the morning I met an old man who lives in one of the Schmidt's units all the time. His '54 Chevy pickup was parked under one of the carports and looked like it would be running for another fifty years. He was sitting at the desk in the window of his room with the curtain opened to let in light. He was writing letters and watching the traffic flow past. He was going to live there, he said, in that little room until he couldn't take care of himself anymore, or until he died.

This is what I didn't do the first night I was there: I didn't call anybody I knew. I didn't go into any shops. I didn't eat at any restaurants.

This is what I did do: I walked.

I walked the length of the main drag and counted the number of new antique stores that had opened since the last time I'd been in Fredericksburg (eleven). I counted the number of Wild West stores (seven), a recent phenomenon that had blossomed since I'd left. I looked at the way that G. Harvey & Son are building a new complex of galleries and shops that are conventional frame buildings, finished with a fake veneer of *fachwork,* the old technique that used to make a little bit of wood go a long way in building by using mud plaster in between timbers. I looked in the window of The African Odyssey, a new shop selling African imports, especially furniture. I saw the billboard map for a planned "garden" complex of stone townhouses near the creek—the advertising rhetoric and the model unit looked like they might fit right in to the suburban areas on the west side of Austin, on the north side of San Antonio, in Houston, in Chicago, etc. I got a feeling for the changes that are transforming this rapidly developing place into even more of a tourist and retirement town.

The first person I ran into that I knew was Brandy Bohton, a man about my own age whom I'd known from the art classes John used to teach. Brandy and Barbara came to Fredericksburg to "settle" down, and they've struggled in a number of jobs to stay there. They sewed curtains, wrote as publicity directors for the local hospital, worked for the Fredericksburg Herb Farm. All the while, Brandy has been diligent about cultivating his position in the community. He is very strongly Christian, and talks often about his faith and about the way that he thanks God for everything good in his life.

Brandy now has his own graphic design/publishing business, with an office in the balcony of the Bank One building. He saw me as I was walking toward Lois's house in the morning, and he stopped backing out his new, gold-colored Blazer and talked to me on the sidewalk for a while. He told me about the way that his publishing venture sort of blossomed around him, driven by a huge boom in local business with a requisite need for graphic design and publication of advertising, brochures, catalogs, etc. He's also now the publisher of a magazine focusing on an "exotic" breed of goat recently introduced into the United States. A few Central Texas ranchers are primary boosters of the goat, and Brandy works with them and other producers to promote the industry in his publication. It's all very slick and seems efficiently done. He took me up to his office, where he's got a scanner, two Power Macs, a laser printer, the whole requisite technology for desktop publishing. He's got an employee, Josiah, whom I know I met when I lived here, but can't remember where.

Brandy and Barbara's life here seems to be an interesting parallel and contrast to my own. They've made a commitment to living in this place and have fought their way into it, trying to find economic stability in the interstices of Fredericksburg's tourist economy. They've been willing to do just about anything, and they've combined that drive with a real entrepreneurial creativity. Now they've got good prospects but the same small rental house with three kids in twelve hundred square feet and five goats in the back yard. Property values are so high right now that they aren't really contemplating buying something else. It's too much of a seller's market right now. Rumors circulate about various Hollywood "glitterati" moving into the area, but not too many people believe them. The local wisdom is that although the area is beautiful, and heritage tourism brings in a lot of people, the region doesn't offer enough other attractions (e.g., skiing, mountains, oceans) to draw and hold the attention of big stars.

Brandy and Barbara are firmly emplaced here, caught up in the fortunes and life of this place as it explodes into something other than the small and relatively sedate town they first encountered.

I wandered around "Alamo Springs" one afternoon after talking with Ollie Kowert about property in the area. Alamo Springs is a former ranch that started being developed as smaller tracts back in the 1970s, and I was wondering what kinds of land might be available there now. Early on, it became a haven for hippies, and a lot of people are still living under somewhat primitive circumstances out there—travel trailers, cobbled-together houses, etc. I found the place on Old Gulf Drive that some acquaintances, Julie and Jerry, told me they had bought. They've been slowly building a small house out there since I left Fredericksburg two years ago. In the last two weeks, they're finally laying some foundation blocks, and they got the electricity turned on a few days ago.

It's a weird piece of property, about a hundred feet wide and a thousand feet long. It extends along the top of a hill, down one side, across a valley bottom, and halfway up another hill. Alamo Springs is a gorgeous piece of Hill Country, cunningly perfect for subdivision development. Lots of narrow canyons and magnificent, distant views, but rocky, rocky, rocky. It's near the old Fredericksburg–San Antonio railroad tunnel that has been converted, by bats, into a huge home for flying mammals, and by the state into a state-controlled wildlife area. At Julie and Jerry's place I ran into a man and woman I had met last year when I went to a local massage therapist's "sweat lodge," but I didn't remember where I knew them from until the end when the woman told me we'd met there. Julie and Jerry arrived around sunset.

Julie told me about her work as a self-employed architect—she's currently working on a several-million-dollar renovation project on a San Saba County ranch. A wealthy German heir is renovating this ranch that he uses only three times a year. He's got two miles of exclusive Colorado River frontage and a huge rock ranchhouse. Julie just got back from Santa Fe and Albuquerque, where she went to "La Puerta," a place that specializes in importing big, ancient doors from the interior of Mexico and from South America so that wealthy patrons can buy them for decorating their houses in the United States. She was supposed to meet her client to buy some doors, but he didn't show up, and she had to choose them herself. She spent $24,000 of his money to buy old doors!

Alamo Springs land seems to be under some cloud of question. The original developers went bankrupt after putting in roads and such, so now the titles are unclear. Some insurance company had liens against the property. It seems like a bit of a paper chase to buy land there—Jerry said he tracked things down through three previous owners and by calling somewhere in New York to find the ownership on the parcel they bought. Even so, a guy who had once been in the process of buying the place in conjunction with someone else showed up one day and camped on the place saying, "This is supposed to be my land." He camped overnight and threatened to burn trees down, but eventually gave up and left. The whole conversation seemed to underscore the paradoxes of trying to live a "local" life in the Hill Country. To find a piece of land, you have to dig through levels of Kafka-esque bureaucracies located far outside the region.

I visited the shack again—like drinking deep from a freshwater spring. Mostly I sat in the sun and just looked and listened. Whoever has bought the neighboring piece of land has put a travel trailer there, and I occasionally heard the sound of power tools coming from that direction. I walked a long way, seven miles down to the river, then back the long way round past Edge Falls and the road toward Clinton Leipner's house. Coming up the hill, a pickup stopped and the driver, Chuck, offered me a ride, and by this time I was pretty tired, so I accepted. He's the person who bought the old Wendenworth place. Though he's young, maybe early forties, he recently retired from teaching philosophy at Trinity University in San Antonio, and now he and his wife live up here. Chuck's worried that the area is going to be developed as a bedroom community for San Antonio.

"It doesn't look like it now, but it'd take a fool not to see what's coming," he said while we sat in his pickup by the gate to my family's place. "All the properties that back up to mine have their fronts out on a blacktop road. You jump on that blacktop and in forty minutes you're at the

Medical Center in downtown San Antonio. It's just a matter of time before this place gets developed. We've been looking for a place in San Saba and Mason Counties. There are still some towns in those places that exist as what they are, not what some developers think they can make of them. Around Llano it's more troublesome—too close to the lakes, Marble Falls and all, but due north in San Saba, and further west in Mason—that's still good country for a decent price; and it's only two or two and a half inches drier in rainfall than here, so you can still try to keep a garden or animals and such."

The author at the "Country Place," also called "The Shack," 1994.
"Somehow ruins give me delight in a crazy way. Maybe writing about them is a way
of restoring; maybe it's an act of restoration . . . or an act of finding the holiness in
the thing that existed. The holiness. The soul of things. . . . Everything falls back into
the earth eventually, and it is a victory to see that story through from beginning to
end. It's a victory to be able to say, 'I'm alive. I can describe it. I can see the story of
the thing from beginning to end and describe its existence.'"—Gerald Stern, in an
interview with Bill Moyers

Closings

BEGINNING AGAIN

When my family tells the story of the ranch, we say we left because we had to—we could not afford to pay the estate taxes after my grandfather's death. This is true, but it is only part of the story. My family left the land because for four generations we had yearned to leave. We had lived in a culture that taught us that a professional life is more respectable than one tied to the land. This attitude shaped the decisions my family made, and it continues to shape the larger political and economic decisions, made by educators and policymakers far removed from the land, that affect the few who still hold on.

My sadness over the loss of the homeplace is my dark side, my grief, but it is also the source of my deepest knowledge. Perhaps it is only through this experience of loss that I can value a sense of place, that I can question how thoughtlessly—even how contemptuously— we are taught to cast it away.

Teresa Jordan, *Riding the White Horse Home:*
A Western Family Album

The story of the German struggle in the Hill Country is finally neither triumphant nor tragic: it is ongoing. It offers more than a momentary insight into America's regional history. It expresses an essential dilemma of a nation's political heritage and the continuing struggle for a truly democratic society. This heritage is a treasury that can be tapped at any time. But to do so it is necessary to avoid romanticizing the past. It then becomes possible to come to terms with its meaning.

Lawrence Goodwyn, *Coming to Terms:*
The German Hill Country of Texas

This is how I wanted to be able to tell the story, how I wanted to be able to live my life:

The aimless, wandering young man discovers his roots in the rural place of his family's heritage. He finds a way to live there, to support himself, his family, and to work for the health of his community. In his wildest fantasy, he even manages to buy the family's original homestead back from the real estate developer who bought it and he turns it into a six-hundred-acre nature preserve with a working farm attached to it. He has many travels in place, lives out a productive life dedicated to sustaining his community and the environment he is a part of, and then walks out into the hills when he is ready to die and returns his body to the vultures and the soil.

This, however, is how the story, my life, is unfolding:

I'm starting at the beginning again for sure. How this is related to anthropology may not be immediately apparent, but it is, and it is related to everything else about me as well. Today is December 4, 1996, and I have not worked on this piece of writing since June 8, 1993. For more than three years, I have lived as silently and unspoken as most lives are most of the time. In that period of silence I have worked as an organic farmer, community activist and organizer, waiter, soil conservationist's assistant, college professor, bead jeweler, and cabinetmaker's apprentice (a one-week gig). . . . Uncle Herbert is gone. Aunt Barbara is gone. Uncle Joe is gone—his face split from a falling hatchet and a steep barn roof and him married again and not to my mom like she wanted. They're all in Nebraska now, along with some of my various cousins—many of them with kids by now. Junior. B.J. Carol. Peeka. Kevin. Wonder whether any of their kids will end up remembering the family's stories like older Syrings? My dad back in Texas again, and me gone again, living in the cold north of Minnesota.

I am both victim and perpetrator in this continued uprooting and wandering. In 1994 and 1995, my life in place became unmoored yet again. The death of John McClusky after a brief, but intense friendship; the birth of my daughter; dissatisfaction with job opportunities in an area rapidly becoming a haven for tourist dollars and little other economic activity; a temporary teaching job offer from my old college; the desire to give my daughter a chance to know and be known by her maternal grandparents; the possibility to farm a piece of land bought by my in-laws—all these things and more pulled me away from the home that Central Texas had become for me and led me, first, back to Iowa (site of my first steps toward adult awareness), then to western Wisconsin / eastern Minnesota where it looks like the next steps of my peripatetic search for relationship to place and community will be taking, well, place.

But place is not something static and independent of a person's position within it. So much has changed in my relationship to place, because so much of my own positioning has changed. That free-floating child, then reclusive teenager, then abstract young man has changed into a father and husband. I was a student; now I'm a sometime teacher. Keith Basso, drawing on his experiences with the Cibecue Apache and the writings of Jean-Paul Sartre, describes this conditional meaning of place:

> Such voices as places possess should not be mistaken for their own.
> Animated by the thoughts and feelings of persons who attend to
> them, places express only what their animators enable them to say;
> like the thirsty sponges to which the philosopher alludes, they yield to
> consciousness only what consciousness has given them to absorb. . . .
> Human constructions par excellence, places consist in what gets made
> of them—in anything and everything they are taken to be—and their
> disembodied voices, immanent though inaudible, are merely those of
> people speaking silently to themselves. (Basso 1996, 108–109)

An image comes to me that my relationship to the concerns of this work—home, place, family, memory—might be compared to the stringing and stitching of beads. Each bead, each mode of understanding, each turn of consciousness, depends on those that precede and those that follow in order to form a pattern, in order to make meaning.

This writing began years ago in a flurry of words and experiences that seem now like a film montage, one thing fading out and the next assuming its place in my attention. Over the years, however, it has remained true to its written medium and become more like a palimpsest—one layer inscribed between and over another, not replacing the previous layer, but emending it, amplifying it, altering it until it becomes neither what was said then, nor what is being said now, but some strange and messy marriage of various times and voices.

Some of the themes that obsessed me back then have sunk into the bedrock of my relationship to the world and this writing. My earlier preoccupation with healing, for instance, especially the attempt to heal the legacy of parental abuse passed from my grandfather to my father, has slipped into the past. Having a child of my own to cherish and nurture has, somewhat unexpectedly, given me the strength and opportunity to overcome much of my own dis-ease. Seeing that I have the capacity to take care of my daughter with love and compassion makes me realize that the past does not, in fact, have to determine the present. Grappling with the memory of painful stories has become a path of healing.

In 1979 Gilbert Jordan (born in 1902), at the urging of his cultural geographer son, published a book, *Yesterday in the Texas Hill Country*, with his reminiscences of growing up in the Hill Country. It is the kind of book you might expect from a nostalgic memoir, full of funny stories, folksy wisdom, and sharp descriptions of a way of life no longer lived by anyone in the region. In prefacing his work, Jordan wrote:

> I write about people of earlier generations and how they lived in houses without modern conveniences; how they rode in buggies, hacks, and wagons; how they shopped in small-town stores; what they did in church and school; how they produced, preserved, and pre-pared their food; how they worked on farms and ranches; what the early artisans accomplished without the aid of modern technology; and what life was like in a bilingual community. The present book is a portrayal of the world of my childhood in the first quarter of our century, and a record of a way of life long past and in part forgotten or unknown. (G. Jordan 1979, xiii)

In many ways, I wish I could write in such a manner, relying on a set of assumptions about how life is a coherent and memorable whole. The fact is, however, I write, somewhat "nervously," about people of my own generation and time—about how we live with modern conveniences and conundrums; how we ride in cars and airplanes almost endlessly between one place and another; how we shop either in cities created as placeless, ahistorical malls, or in towns self-consciously constructed as touristy "places"; what we do with a history treated like "church"; how we no longer live nor work on farms and ranches; how everything we accomplish is mediated by modern technology; what life is like in a problematic world of questions regarding our places. This present book is a record of a way of life struggling to weave a whole for itself out of the dreams and fragments of stories and experience that have been its lot in the last quarter of our century.

Jordan concludes his book:

Fortunately a new impetus to the preservation of the various cultures of our state has come from a recently awakened concern over the state's diverse ethnic groups and their contributions to our common cultural heritage. . . . It is the author's hope that the present book will contribute to this new trend. (1979, 162)

My own conclusion is less idealistic, perhaps:

It is my hope that this book evokes the way that a grappling with questions of family, place, home, and stories might open a path toward creating a meaningful, gathered life in a chaotic time.

Bibliography

Agnew, John A., and James S. Duncan, eds.
1989   *The Power of Place: Bringing Together Geographical and Sociological Imaginations.*
        Boston: Unwin Hyman.

Allen, Barbara, and Thomas J. Schlereth, eds.
1990   *Sense of Place: American Regional Cultures.* Lexington: University of Kentucky
        Press.

Altman, Irwin, and Setha M. Low, eds.
1992   *Place Attachment. Human Behavior and Environment: Advances in Theory and
        Research,* vol. 12. New York: Plenum Press.

Anderson, Ernest Leon
1987   *Scraping By: A Field Study of Semi-Rural Poverty in the Texas Hill Country.* Diss.,
        University of Texas at Austin.

Anzaldua, Gloria
1987   *Borderlands/La Frontera: The New Mestiza.* San Francisco: aunt lute books.

Bachelard, Gaston
1964   *The Poetics of Space.* New York: Orion Press.

Bammer, Angelika, ed.
1994   *Displacements: Cultural Identities in Question.* Bloomington: Indiana University
        Press.

Barnes, Trevor J., and James D. Duncan, eds.
1992   *Writing Worlds: Discourse, Text and Metaphor in the Representation of Landscape.*
        London: Routledge.

Bass, Rick
1985   *The Deer Pasture.* New York: W. W. Norton & Co.

Basso, Keith
1996   *Wisdom Sits in Places: Landscape and Language among the Western Apache.* Albuquerque: University of New Mexico Press.

Basso, Keith, and Steven Feld, eds.
1996   *Senses of Place.* Santa Fe: School of American Research Press.

Batteau, Allen
1983   *Appalachia and America: Autonomy and Regional Dependence.* Lexington: University of Kentucky Press.

Bauman, Richard.
1986   *Story, Performance, and Event.* New York: Cambridge University Press.

Beaver, Patricia D.
1986   *Rural Community in the Appalachian South.* Lexington: University of Kentucky Press.

Berry, Wendell
1977   *The Unsettling of America: Culture and Agriculture.* San Francisco: Sierra Club Books.
1990   "The Work of Local Culture." In *What Are People For?*, 153–169. London: Rider Books.

Bode, Elroy
1983   *This Favored Place: The Texas Hill Country.* Bryan, TX: Shearer Publishing.

Bodnar, John
1992   *Remaking America: Public Memory, Commemoration, and Patriotism in the Twentieth Century.* Princeton: Princeton University Press.

Bommes, Michael, and Patrick Wright
1982   "'Charms of residence': The Public and the Past." In *Making Histories: Studies in History-Writing and Politics,* 253–302. Minneapolis: University of Minnesota Press.

Boym, Svetlana
1996   "Unsettling Homecoming." In *Fieldwork: Sites in Literary and Cultural Studies,* ed. Marjorie Garber et al., 262–267. New York: Routledge.

Brown, Barbara, and Douglas D. Perkins
1992   "Disruptions in Place Attachment." In *Place Attachment*, ed. Irwin Altman and Setha M. Low, 279–303. New York: Plenum Press.

Bryant, F. C.
1981   *We're All Kin: A Cultural Study of a Mountain Neighborhood.* Knoxville: University of Tennessee Press.

Buchanan, Rita
1987   *A Weaver's Garden.* Loveland, CO: Interweave Press.

Buttimer, Anne
1980   "Home, Reach, and the Sense of Place." In *The Human Experience of Space and Place,* ed. Anne Buttimer and David Seamon, 166–187. New York: St. Martin's Press.

Buttimer, Anne, and David Seamon, eds.
1980   *The Human Experience of Space and Place.* New York: St. Martin's Press.

Campion, William J.
1975   *The Lore and Legend of the Texas Hill Country.* Fredericksburg, TX: Private publication.

Carmack, R. M.
1972   "Ethnohistory: A Review of Its Development, Definitions, Methods, and Aims." *Annual Review of Anthropology 1972:* 227–246.

Carroll, Peter N.
1990   *Keeping Time: Memory, Nostalgia, and the Art of History.* Athens: University of Georgia Press.

Carter, Keith
1990   *The Blue Man: Photographs.* Houston: Rice University Press.

Casey, Edward
1987   "The World of Nostalgia." *Man and World* 20:361–384.
1993   *Getting Back into Place: Toward a Renewed Understanding of the Place-World.* Bloomington: University of Indiana Press.

Cisneros, Sandra
1991   *Woman Hollering Creek and Other Stories.* New York: Random House.

Cook, Sylvia Rusche
1975   *The Rock Houses of Fredericksburg, Texas, 1846–1910.* Thesis, University of New Mexico.

Cosgrove, Denis, and Stephen Daniels, eds.
1988   *The Iconography of Landscape: Essays on the Symbolic Representation, Design, and Use of Past Environments.* Cambridge: Cambridge University Press.

Cragg, Barbara
1982   "Wild Daniel's Farm: A Family Geography." *Landscape* 26(2): 41–48.

Daniels, John
1992   *The Trail Home.* New York: Pantheon Books.

Dietrich, Katheryn Ann
1994   *Reproduction of Collective Ethnic Identity in a German American Community.* Diss., Texas A&M University.

Dillon, David
1993   "Deep in the Heart." *Historic Preservation* 45(5): 28–37.

Doughty, Robin W.
1987   *At Home in Texas: Early Views of the Land.* College Station: Texas A&M University Press.

Entrikin, J. Nicholas
1991   *The Betweenness of Place: Towards a Geography of Modernity.* Houndsmill: Macmillan.

Erdrich, Louise
1988   "A Writer's Sense of Place." In *A Place of Sense: Essays in Search of the Midwest,* ed. Michael Martone, 34–44. Iowa City: University of Iowa Press.

Evans-Pritchard, E. E.
1962   "Anthropology and History." In *Essays in Social Anthropology,* 46–65. London: Faber and Faber.

Fischer, Michael M. J.
1986   "Ethnicity and the Postmodern Arts of Memory." In *Writing Culture: The Poetics and Politics of Ethnography,* ed. James Clifford and George Marcus, 194–233. Berkeley: University of California Press.

Foster, Stephen William

1988   *The Past Is Another Country: Representation, Historical Consciousness, and Resistance in the Blue Ridge.* Berkeley: University of California Press.

Fowler, Peter J.

1992   *The Past in Contemporary Society: Then, Now.* London: Routledge.

Frank, Geyla

1979   "Finding the Common Denominator: A Phenomenological Critique of the Life History Method." *Ethos* 7(1): 169–194.

Fredericksburg Chamber of Commerce

1964   *Fredericksburg: In the Texas Hill Country.* Fredericksburg, TX: Fredericksburg Chamber of Commerce.

Garber, Marjorie, Rebecca L. Walkowitz, and Paul B. Franklin, eds.

1996   *Fieldwork: Sites in Literary and Cultural Studies.* New York: Routledge.

Garrett, George

1990   "Uncles and Others." In *Located Lives: Place and Idea in Southern Autobiography,* ed. J. Bill Berry, 132–151. Athens: University of Georgia Press.

Gillespie County Historical Society

1960   *Pioneers in God's Hills,* vol. 1, *Stories and Biographies.* Austin: Von Boeckmann-Jones.

1974   *Pioneers in God's Hills,* vol. 2, *A History of Fredericksburg and Gillespie County People and Events.* Austin: Von Boeckmann-Jones.

Gish, Theodore, and Richard Spuler, eds.

1986   *Eagle in the New World: German Immigration to Texas and America.* College Station: Texas A&M Press.

Glasscock, Judith

1992   "On the Antiques Trail." *An Insider's Guide to the Texas Hills* (fall/winter): 27–28.

Graves, John

1960   *Goodbye to a River.* New York: Knopf.

1973   *Hard Scrabble: Observations on a Patch of Land.* New York: Knopf.

1980   *From a Limestone Ledge: Some Essays and Other Ruminations about Country Life in Texas.* New York: Knopf.

Greene, A. G.

1972   *The Last Captive.* Austin: Encino Press.

Gruchow, Paul
1995   *Grassroots: The Universe of Home.* Minneapolis: Milkweed Editions.

Haar, Michel
1993   *The Song of the Earth: Heidegger and the Grounds of the History of Being,* trans. Reginald Lilly. Bloomington: Indiana University Press.

Haas, Oscar
1968   *History of New Braunfels and Comal County, Texas: 1844–1946.* Austin: Steck Co.

Hahn, Emily
1991   "Profiles: A Place and an Attitude." *The New Yorker,* January 21, 64–76.

Hale, Leon
1989   *Texas Chronicles.* Fredericksburg, TX: Shearer Publishing.

Handler, Richard, and William Saxton
1988   "Dyssimulation: Reflexivity, Narrative, and the Quest for Authenticity in 'Living History.'" *Cultural Anthropology* 3(3): 247–260.

Haraway, Donna
1988   "Situated Knowledges: The Science Question in Feminism and the Privilege of Partial Perspective." *Feminist Studies* 14:575–599.

Hareven, Tamara, and Randolph Langenbach
1981   "Living Places, Work Places, and Historical Identity." In *Our Past before Us: Why Do We Save It?* ed. David Lowenthal and Marcus Binney, 109–123. London: Temple Smith.

Harper, Ralph
1966   *Nostalgia: An Existential Exploration of Longing and Fulfillment in the Modern Age.* Cleveland: Press of Western Reserve University.

Heartland Network
1994   *Heartland Voices,* vol. 1, No. 1: "Changing Places, Changing People: Texas Hill Country Residents Share Ideas about the Region and Its Future."

Heat-Moon, William Least
1991   *Prairyerth: A Deep Map.* Boston: Houghton Mifflin Co.

Heidegger, Martin
1971   "Building Dwelling Thinking." In *Poetry, Language, Thought,* trans. Albert Hofstadter. New York: Harper and Row.

Herbert, David T.
1990   *Cities in Space: City as Place.* Savage, MD: Barnes and Noble.

Hermann, Maria
1977   "The Restoration of Historic Fredericksburg." In *Texas and Germany: Cross-currents,* ed. Joseph Wilson, 119–139. Houston: William Marsh Rice University.

Hiss, Tony
1990   *The Experience of Place.* New York: Knopf.

Hobsbawm, Eric, and Terence Ranger, eds.
1983   *The Invention of Tradition.* Cambridge and New York: Cambridge University Press.

Hosmer, Charles.
1981   *Preservation Comes of Age: From Williamsburg to the National Trust.* Charlottesville: University Press of Virginia.

Johnstone, Barbara
1990   *Stories, Community, and Place: Narratives from Middle America.* Bloomington: Indiana University Press.

Jordan, Gilbert J.
1979   *Yesterday in the Texas Hill Country.* College Station: Texas A&M University Press.
1980   *German Texana: A Bilingual Collection of Traditional Materials.* Burnet, TX: Eakin Press.

Jordan, Teresa
1993   *Riding the White Horse Home: A Western Family Album.* New York: Vintage Books.

Jordan, Terry G.
1966   *German Seed in Texas Soil: Immigrant Farmers in Nineteenth-Century Texas.* Austin: University of Texas Press.
1964   "German Houses in Texas." *Landscape* 14 (autumn): 24–26.

Kammen, Michael
1987   *Selvages and Biases: The Fabric of History in American Culture.* Ithaca: Cornell University Press.
1991   *Mystic Chords of Memory: The Transformation of Tradition in American History.* New York: Knopf.

Kemmis, Daniel
1990 *Community and the Politics of Place.* Norman: University of Oklahoma Press.

King, Thomas F., Patricia Parker Hickman, and Gary Berg
1977 *Anthropology in Historic Preservation: Caring for Culture's Clutter.* New York: Academic Press.

Kluckhohn, Clyde
1945 "The Personal Document in Anthropological Science." In *The Use of Personal Documents in History, Anthropology, and Sociology,* ed. Louis Reichenthal Gottschalk, 79–175. Social Science Research Council Bulletin 53.

Kowert, Elise
1977 *Old Homes and Buildings of Fredericksburg.* Fredericksburg, TX: Fredericksburg Publishing Company.
1980 *Historic Homes in and around Fredericksburg.* Fredericksburg, TX: Fredericksburg Publishing Company.

Langnes, L. L., and Gelya Frank
1986 *Lives: An Anthropological Approach to Biography.* Novato, CA: Chandler and Sharp.

Lasch, Christopher
1991 "Nostalgia: The Abdication of Memory." In *The True and Only Heaven: Progress and Its Critics,* 82–119. New York: W. W. Norton & Co.

Lehmann, George
1972 *Nine Years among the Indians, 1870–1879.* Austin: Von Boeckmann-Jones.

Lich, Glen E.
1981 *The German Texans.* San Antonio: University of Texas Institute of Texan Cultures.
1986 "Rural Hill Country: Man, Nature, and the Ecological Perspective." In *Eagle in the New World,* ed. Theodore Gish and Richard Spuler, 26–46. College Station: Texas A&M Press.

Lich, Glen E., and Dona B. Reeves-Marquardt, eds.
1978 *German Culture in Texas: A Free Earth; Essays from the 1978 Southwest Symposium.* Boston: Twayne Publishers.
1986 *Texas Country: The Changing Rural Scene.* College Station: Texas A&M University Press.

Lindig, Otto
1970 *100 Years: Historical Recollections of Gillespie County, 1870–1970.* Stonewall, TX.

Lippard, Lucy R.
1997   *The Lure of the Local: Senses of Place in a Multicentered Society.* New York: New Press.

Lipsitz, George
1990   *Time Passages: Collective Memory and American Popular Culture.* Minneapolis: University of Minnesota Press.

Lopez, Barry
1988   "Landscape and Narrative." In *Crossing Open Ground,* 61–71. New York: Charles Scribner's Sons.
1989   "The American Geographies." *Orion Nature Quarterly* 8(4): 52–61.

Low, Setha M., and Denise L. Lawrence
1990   "The Built Environment and Spatial Form." *Annual Review of Anthropology,* 453–505.

Lowenthal, David
1975   "Past Time, Present Place: Landscape and Memory." *Geographical Review* 65(1): 1–24.
1985   *The Past Is a Foreign Country.* Cambridge: Cambridge University Press.

Lowenthal, David, and Marcus Binney, eds.
1981   *Our Past before Us: Why Do We Save It?* London: Temple Smith.

Lukacs, John
1985   *Historical Consciousness; or, The Remembered Past.* New York: Schocken Books.

MacCannell, Dean
1976   *The Tourist: A New Theory of the Leisure Class.* New York: Schocken Books.
1992   *Empty Meeting Grounds: The Tourist Papers.* London: Routledge.

Macfarlane, Alan
1977   *Reconstructing Historical Communities.* London: Cambridge University Press.

Marcus, Claire Cooper
1992   "Environmental Memories." In *Place Attachment,* ed. Irwin Altman and Setha Low, 87–112. *Human Behavior and Environment: Advances in Theory and Research,* vol. 12. New York: Plenum Press.

Massey, Doreen
1994   "Double Articulation: A Place in the World." In *Displacements: Cultural Identities in Question,* ed. Angelika Bammer, 110–121. Bloomington: Indiana University Press.

Martinello, Marian L., with Ophelia Nielsen Weinheimer

1987   *The Search for Emma's Story: A Model for Humanities Detective Work.* Fort Worth: Texas Christian University Press.

Miller, Ray

1980   *Eyes of Texas Travel Guide: Hill Country/Permian Basin Edition.* Houston: Cordovan Corporation.

Moursund, John Stribling

1979   *Blanco County History.* Burnet, TX: Nortex Press.

Murtagh, William J.

1988   *Keeping Time: The History and Theory of Preservation in America.* Pittstown, NJ: Main Street Press.

Nabhan, Gary Paul

1997   *Cultures of Habitat: On Nature, Culture, and Story.* Washington, DC: Counterpoint.

Naficy, Hamid

1981   "The Poetics and Practice of Iranian Nostalgia." *Diaspora* 1(3): 285–382.

Narayan, Kirin

1993   "How Native Is a 'Native' Anthropologist?" *American Anthropologist* 95(3): 671–686.

Parabola

1993   "Place and Space." Special Issue, 18(2).

Pederson, Jane Marie

1992   *Between Memory and Reality: Family and Community in Rural Wisconsin, 1870–1970.* Madison: University of Wisconsin Press.

Penniger, Robert

1971   *Fredericksburg, Texas . . . The First Fifty Years.* Fredericksburg, TX: Fredericksburg Publishing Company.

Perry, Garland A.

1982   *Historic Images of Boerne, Texas.* Boerne, TX.

Phelan, Richard

1976   *Texas Wild: The Land, Plants, and Animals of the Lone Star State.* New York: Dutton.

Pocius, Gerald L.
1991   *A Place to Belong: Community Order and Everyday Space in Calvert, Newfound-
land.* Athens: University of Georgia Press.

Popular Memory Group
1982   "Popular Memory: Theory, Politics, Method." In *Making Histories: Studies in
History-Writing and Politics,* 205–252. Minneapolis: University of Minnesota
Press.

Ransleben, Guido E.
1954   *A Hundred Years of Comfort in Texas: A Centennial History.* San Antonio: Nay-
lor Company.

Relph, Edward
1976   *Place and Placelessness.* London: Pion Press.

Richardson, Laural
1995   "Narrative and Sociology." In *Representation in Ethnography,* ed. John Van Maa-
nen, 198–221. Thousand Oaks, CA: Sage Publications.

Roach, Joyce Gibson, ed.
1992   *This Place of Memory: A Texas Perspective.* Denton: University of North Texas
Press.

Robertson, George, Melinda Mash, Lisa Tickner, Jon Bird, Barry Curtis, and Tim Put-
nam, eds.
1992   *Travellers' Tales: Narratives of Home and Displacement.* London: Routledge.

Rosaldo, Renato
1980   *Ilongot Headhunting, 1883–1974: A Study in Society and History.* Stanford: Stanford University Press.

Rosen, George
1975   "Nostalgia: A 'Forgotten' Psychological Disorder." *Clio Medica* 10(1): 28–51.

Roth, Michael S.
1991   "Dying of the Past: Medical Studies of Nostalgia in Nineteenth-Century
France." *History and Memory* 3(1): 5–29.

Ryden, Kent C.
1993   *Mapping the Invisible Landscape: Folklore, Writing, and the Sense of Place.* Iowa
City: University of Iowa Press.

Sahlins, Marshall
1985   *Islands of History.* Chicago: University of Chicago Press.

Sanders, Scott Russell
1993   *Staying Put: On Making a Home in a Restless World.* Boston: Beacon Press.

Sarris, Greg
1993   *Keeping Slugwoman Alive: A Holistic Approach to American Indian Texts.* Berkeley: University of California Press.

Sarup, Madan
1992   "Home and Identity." In *Travellers' Tales: Narratives of Home and Displacement,* ed. George Robertson et al., 93–104. London: Routledge.

Schneider, David M.
1980   *American Kinship: A Cultural Account,* 2d ed. Chicago: University of Chicago Press.

Schumaker, Sally A., and Gerald J. Conti
1985   "Understanding Mobility in America: Conflicts between Stability and Change." In *Home Environments,* ed. Irwin Altman and Carol M. Werner, 237–253. *Human Behavior and Environment: Advances in Theory and Research,* vol. 8. New York: Plenum Press.

Seamon, David, and Robert Mugerauer, eds.
1985   *Dwelling, Place, and Environment: Towards a Phenomenology of Person and World.* Dordrecht (Netherlands): Kluwer Academic Publishers.

Shudson, Michael
1992   *Watergate in American Memory.* New York: Basic Books.

Simic, Charles
1985   *The Uncertain Certainty: Interviews, Essays, and Notes on Poetry.* Ann Arbor: University of Michigan Press.

Smith, Valene L., ed.
1989   *Hosts and Guests: The Anthropology of Tourism,* 2d ed. Philadelphia: University of Pennsylvania Press.

Stanush, Michele
1993   "Hill Country Treasures: Group Works to Preserve One of 'Last Great Places'." *Austin American-Statesman,* June 6, E6, E13.

Stegner, Wallace
1992   *Where the Bluebird Sings to the Lemonade Springs: Living and Writing in the West.*
        New York: Penguin Books.

Stewart, Kathleen
1992   "Nostalgia—A Polemic." In *Rereading Cultural Anthropology,* ed. George Marcus, 252–266. Durham, NC: Duke University Press.
1995   *A Space on the Side of the Road: Cultural Politics in an "Other" America.* Princeton: Princeton University Press.

Snyder, Gary
1990   "The Place, the Region, and the Commons." In *The Practice of the Wild,* 25–47. San Francisco: North Point Press.
1996   *A Place in Space: Ethics, Aesthetics, and Watersheds.* Washington, DC: Counterpoint.

Tedlock, Dennis
1983   "Learning to Listen: Oral History as Poetry." In *The Spoken Word and the Work of Interpretation,* 107–123. Philadelphia: University of Pennsylvania Press.

Tetzlaff, Otto W.
1977   "A Guide for German Immigrants." In *Texas and Germany: Crosscurrents,* ed. Joseph Wilson, 13–19. Houston: William Marsh Rice University.

Trinh T., Minh-ha
1989   *Woman Native Other.* Bloomington: Indiana University Press.

Tuan, Yi-Fu
1974   *Topophilia: A Study of Environmental Perception, Attitudes, and Values.* Englewood Cliffs, NJ: Prentice-Hall.
1977   *Space and Place: The Perspective of Experience.* Minneapolis: University of Minnesota Press.
1980   "Rootedness versus Sense of Place." *Landscape* 24(1): 3–8.

Washington, Mary Helen, ed.
1991   *Memory of Kin: Stories about Family by Black Writers.* New York: Doubleday.

Watriss, Wendy, and Fred Baldwin
1991   *Coming to Terms: The German Hill Country of Texas.* College Station: Texas A&M University Press.

Watson, Lawrence C., and Maria-Barbara Watson-Franke
1985   *Interpreting Life Histories: An Anthropological Inquiry.* New Brunswick, NJ: Rutgers University Press.

Whisnant, David E.

1980 *Modernizing the Mountaineer: People, Power, and Planning in Appalachia.* New York: Burt Franklin & Co.

1983 *All That Is Native and Fine: The Politics of Culture in an American Region.* Chapel Hill: University of North Carolina Press.

White, Hayden

1978 *Tropics of Discourse: Essays in Cultural Criticism.* Baltimore: Johns Hopkins University Press.

White, J. Roy

1968 *Limestone and Log: A Hill Country Sketchbook.* Text by Joseph B. Frantz. Austin: Encino Press.

Williams, Terry Tempest

1991 *Refuge: An Unnatural History of Family and Place.* New York: Pantheon Books.

Wilson, Joseph, ed.

1977 *Texas and Germany: Crosscurrents.* Rice University Studies 63(3). Houston: William Marsh Rice University.

Wimberley, C. W.

1988 *Cedar Whacker: Stories of the Texas Hill Country.* Austin: Eakin Press.

Wood, Susan

1991 *Campo Santo.* Baton Rouge: Louisiana State University Press.

Zinsser, William, ed.

1987 *Inventing the Truth: The Art and Craft of Memoir.* Boston: Houghton Mifflin.